head
heart
crotch
connections

How Not to Fail in Search of Your
Perfect Union

René Gilberto Vázquez del Valle, DSW, LCSW-R

Copyright © 2022 by Dr. René Gilberto Vázquez del Valle Head, Heart, Crotch Connections: How Not to Fail in Search of Your Perfect Union

All rights reserved. No part of this publication may be reproduced, distributed, or transmitted in any form or by any means, including photocopying, recording, or other electronic or mechanical methods, without the prior written permission of the publisher, except in the case of brief quotations embodied in critical reviews and certain other noncommercial uses permitted by copyright law.

Although the author and publisher have made every effort to ensure that the information in this book was correct at press time, the author and publisher do not assume and hereby disclaim any liability to any party for any loss, damage, or disruption caused by errors or omissions, whether such errors or omissions result from negligence, accident, or any other cause.

Neither the author nor the publisher assumes any responsibility or liability whatsoever on behalf of the consumer or reader of this material. Any perceived slight of any individual or organization is purely unintentional.

The resources in this book are provided for informational purposes only and should not be used to replace the specialized training and professional judgment of any guidance, school, or college counselor.

Neither the author nor the publisher can be held responsible for the use of the information provided within this book. This book is intended to help give guidance and assistance to the best of the author's ability. Please use your own best judgment when making your college-planning decisions.

This work depicts actual events in the life of the author as truthfully as recollection permits. All persons within are actual individuals; there are no composite characters. The names of all individuals have been changed to respect their privacy.

ISBN (paperback): 979-8-88759-024-0

ISBN (eBook): 979-8-88759-025-7

Cover design by

Printed in the U.S.A

This book is in memory of David, Robert, and Tony and is dedicated to my good friends, Arthur, Agnes, Adiel, Anthony/Arthur, and my nephew, Dr. Juan David Rivera, DSW, who continue to inspire me.

I am so glad you bought my book! I'd like to offer you a free gift, my *"Head, Heart, Crotch Connection Scale"* for you to utilize. It will quickly help you identify the strongest and weakest link in your romantic connection by highlighting the area of vulnerability in your attachment that requires more attention.

Head on over to my website, <u>renev.authorchannel.co</u> to claim yours today!

Author's Note

Head, Heart, Crotch Connections is a self-help book about relational psychology, which focuses on the areas of human functioning (aspects of the mind, body, and spirit) that can be explored, understood, and improved upon when an individual wishes to achieve a better intimate relationship. This book is a formulaic account of how to identify the type of intimate connection you have in your relationship, the level of attachment it sustains, and how to overcome the difficulties that come with creating a more perfect union.

Relationships often fail, as evidenced by the high rate of divorce and the vast quantity of books on how best to improve your relationship. Authors with best-selling books such as Gary Chapman's book, *The 5 Love Languages: The Secret to Love That Lasts,* Marcus and Ashley Kusi's book, *Emotional and Sexual Intimacy in Marriage: How to Connect or Reconnect With Your Spouse, Grow Together, and Strengthen Your Marriage,* and Dr. Love and Dr. Stosny's book, *How to Improve Your Marriage Without Talking About It,* all offer extensive, knowledgeable information on how best to improve a relationship. The prevalence of a vast number of books on how best to improve your relationship demonstrates how common conflicts in relationships are and the need to actively work on improving them for success.

Head, Heart, Crotch Connections

According to Dr. Alan Hawkins, a renowned psychologist who created a website entitled "YourDivorceQuestions.org," researchers have estimated that a significant number of first marriages in the US—roughly 50 percent—will end in divorce or permanent separation, while about 60-65 percent of second marriages end in divorce.[1]

Relationships fail more often than they succeed, but why they fail can remain elusive and hidden away or, for many, even shameful to talk about. Much is known about the difficulties in relationships, but comparatively, little is written which characterizes what accounts for attachment, how attachment leads to connections, and how disruptions in connections can lead to the dissolution of a relationship. There is also little written that identifies how problems in connection often occur when we limit the expression of words. This book focuses on how to utilize words to explain your thoughts, emotions, and sexual perceptions to create the experience of attachment. It has been my experience that connections can be altered and relationships can prevail, despite the aforementioned dwindling rates of success.

It is with the hope of demystifying and de-stigmatizing failure in relationships that I share my thoughts on this topic. I expect it will be a journey of discovery and exploration of the inner operations of the head, heart, and crotch.

---

1   Dr. Alan Hawkins, "How Common Is Divorce and What Are the Reasons?: Your Divorce Questions," Your Divorce Questions |, May 23, 2016, http://yourdivorcequestions.org/how-common-is-divorce/.

Table of Contents

Introduction 11
CHAPTER 1
What I Mean by "Head, Heart, Crotch Connection" 15
    Why Psychotherapy Can Help 18
    Unconscious Connections 19
    Identifying Your Connection Preference 20
CHAPTER 2
What is a Head Connection? 21
    Determine Shared Values vs. Conflicting Values 22
    Examine Your Values 23
    The Value of Empathy 24
Additional Resources to Explore Your Values 25
CHAPTER 3
What Is a Heart Connection? 27
CHAPTER 4
What Is a Crotch Connection? 31
    Love (Attachment) 33
    Overcoming Obstacles 35
CHAPTER 5
Words Create Experience 37
    The 6 W's of Connection: Who, Why, What, Which,
    Where, and When 37
    Discussing the Head, Heart, Crotch Connection 38
    Putting Words to Experience 39
    Experiences Create Attachment 41

    Relating to the Full Person 42

CHAPTER 6
The Head, Heart, Crotch Connection Is Like a Puzzle. 45

    Polar Opposite 46

CHAPTER 7
Why a Relationship Can Fail 49

    Demise of the Head Connection 49

    Demise of the Heart Connection 50

CHAPTER 8
The Importance of a Head, Heart, Crotch Connection. 55

    Addressing Missing Pieces 56

    Appreciating the Value of Connection 57

CHAPTER 9
What Affects Success?. 61

    Where Fantasy and Flight Works but for a While 62

    Importance of Separateness 64

CHAPTER 10
When and How to Address Your Current Head, Heart, Crotch Connection 65

    The Heart Connection: Empathy and Sensitivity 66

    Danger Signs. 67

    How Self-Esteem Affects Outcomes 68

    Sexual Connection 69

CHAPTER 11
When Does a Relationship Begin to Fail? 71

    How the Head Connection Fails 72

    How the Heart Connection Fails 72

    How the Crotch Connection Fails 73

CHAPTER 12
Denial: Heads in the Sand................................. 75

CHAPTER 13
Why Do Words Matter?..................................... 77
    Exploring the Sexual Connection...................... 79

CHAPTER 14
When Familiarity Breeds Contempt........................ 85

CHAPTER 15
Not All Connections Are Created Equal 89
    The Importance of Exploring Connections Fully 90

CHAPTER 16
What Is the Nature of Your Head, Heart, Crotch Connection? .. 95
    Importance of Identifying the Nature of Your Attachment .. 98

CHAPTER 17
When Trauma Affects Our HHC Connection................ 101
    Determine If Your HHC Connection Is Positive or Negative 102
    The Benefits of Exploring the HHC Connection.......... 103

CHAPTER 18
What's Needed to Make a Good Head, Heart, Crotch Connection? 107
    Overcoming Disconnection and Addressing the Area of Vulnerability in Your Relationship 108
    What Mental Representations Are You Holding Onto?.... 110
    Substantive Words for a Better Attachment............. 112
    Rating Scale to Determine Level of Connection 113
    Guide to Interpreting Rating Scale.................... 113

CHAPTER 19
Why Does Age Affect Our Perception of a Head, Heart, Crotch Connection? 117

Appendix A: List of Common Values..................... 119

Appendix B: List of Feelings Experienced 121
Appendix C: Description of Healthy Sexual Feelings 123
Recommended Reading 125
Acknowledgments................................... 129
About the Author 131

Introduction

The premise that the connections made at the level of the head, heart, and crotch figuratively could be assessed developed from my practice of 40 years of psychotherapy, with individuals and couples, as a clinical social worker. After receiving my doctoral degree and upon retiring in Dec 2010 from a New York State Office of Mental Health position, working within an outpatient clinic, I had the time and desire to write about my clinical work with patients in therapy who had experienced relationship difficulties.

Two years later, in 2012, I started writing down my ideas. The ideas I wish to impart and share with you are based purely on my clinical work with patients in the outpatient mental health clinic and with clients from my private practice and are not based on research. I came to believe that a book on this topic would be helpful from my work in helping patients understand what was occurring in

Head, Heart, Crotch Connections

their relationships, how they were relating to their partners, and observing how their relationships either evolved or failed to thrive.

For me personally, it was often heart-wrenching to watch and see my clients describe their situations and not be able to intervene to help alleviate their suffering. It wasn't until I started exploring with them this yet underdeveloped hypothesis on how the head, heart, crotch triune functions that I realized how it functioned in their lives. When I utilize the words "head, heart, crotch," I am referring to the mind, spirit, and sexual energy, also known as libido, to explain connections made in intimate relationships. "Head connection" refers to the mind's thoughts, "heart connection" refers to the feelings often associated with the spirit or the heart, and "crotch connection" refers to libidinal energy and its use in your relationship.

In work with my clients, I would often explain the "head, heart, crotch" concept to them and ask them to allow me to explore these areas of their life to see if they understood it, and if it somehow resonated and made sense to them. The more they would allow me to explore their connections, the more I was able to clarify for them the struggles they were having in identifying the failures in connection that occurred. Their willingness to look at their failures in connection often helped them overcome the dysfunction in their relationship. As I pursued my theory, I noticed drastic changes in how my clients would relate to their partners and how it would prevent sudden disconnections and ruptures in their unions. As I further developed this technique, it appeared to achieve greater success.

Intending to share my work, I put forward my thoughts on how exploring and reflecting on the connections at the levels of "head, heart, and crotch" works to overcome struggles in maintaining intimacy and attachment. It is ultimately with the desire to write a series of books on how relationships can possibly fail and how to overcome this potential failure that I journal my experiences with psychotherapy and share the joy and pain in the lives of the people I was entrusted to help.

When finished with this book, you will:
- fully understand the head, heart, crotch connection.
- have the tools needed to assess your relationship properly.
- determine steps needed to improve your relationship.
- learn how communication is key to your relationship.
- understand why relationships can fail and how to avoid pitfalls.

I truly look forward to helping you find joy in your head, heart, crotch connection.

Dr. René Gilberto Vázquez del Valle

CHAPTER 1

What I Mean by "Head, Heart, Crotch Connection"

The head, heart, crotch connection refers to those aspects of an interpersonal relationship that, when examined, can help determine if strong connections are being made. It can also help explain how a lack of fulfillment in certain areas of one's mental, emotional, and sexual world may lead to dissatisfaction within a relationship. It can also point to the reasons behind a relationship's possible demise.

You may be asking yourself why a self-help book on relationships starts out by explaining how not to *fail* in relationships. The answer is because that would be a very good place to start. Statistically, we know that over 50 percent of marriages end in separation or divorce. Yet, this staggering statistic doesn't automatically translate into any sense of what actually goes wrong in relationships; it merely informs us that we are, in some strange way, doomed to fail—or that the greater chance for success is out of our control and is more of a matter of chance.

In 2014, according to the American Psychological Association, infidelity was cited as the primary cause of divorce in 25-40 percent of divorces.[2] The Kinsey Institute at Indiana University, which for 75 years has been a trusted source for scientific research on issues in sexuality and gender, notes that in western countries, approximately 20-25 percent of men and 10-19 percent of women engage in extramarital sex at least once.[3] That may seem like one clear answer, but infidelity alone is not the only cause of divorce—as we've seen, it is only the primary cause in 25-40 percent of them.

That said, an extramarital affair does cause significant disruptions in relationships. The influence an extramarital affair has on maintaining intimacy and how it leads to physical or emotional disconnection can be affected by one's ability to communicate effectively.

As a result, it has occurred to me that, in a world where we are ever more connected to multiple means of communication, we may actually be experiencing more struggles in intimacy. We are communicating and understanding less nowadays. With social media, we have multiple means of accessing connections and speaking with others—but we also have multiple technologies we can constantly check to see if they have rejected us. Rejection is the fastest way of feeling disconnected.

Technological disconnections lead me to believe that we are clearly talking more but may be communicating less. This is also evidenced by our ability to disconnect from one another so easily. The new, broader forms of communication often lack depth, but we can fail to see the absence of substance when we are so used to relating to one another so superficially. Because we now often speak in sound bytes and snip-its, we often fail to truly communicate all our thoughts at deeper levels. It is as if relating superficially is becoming the norm,

---

[2] Gabrielle Applebury, "Infidelity Statistics on Men, Women, and Relationships," Gabrielle assisted families with co-parenting after a divorce (LoveToKnow, 2022), https://divorce.lovetoknow.com/Rates_of_Divorce_for_Adultery_and_Infidelity.

[3] Kristen P. Mark, Erick Janssen, and Robin R. Milhausen, "Infidelity in Heterosexual Couples: Demographic, Interpersonal, and Personality-Related Predictors of Extradyadic Sex," Archives of Sexual Behavior 40, no. 5 (November 2011): pp. 971-982, https://doi.org/10.1007/s10508-011-9771-z.

CHAPTER 1

and we fail to see the inherent danger it holds for creating intimate connections.

Likewise, it can induce attachment disruptions when we fail to communicate, relate only superficially, and disconnect so quickly. We can now fail to create genuine intimacy because we disconnect so easily when utilizing social media forums such as Facebook, Instagram, Twitter, and TikTok. In my clinical practice, many clients informed me of how their relationship may have ended or how they lost their sense of connection when they communicated mainly through social media, in the form of texts, chats, and videos, as opposed to in-person communication. Many clients admitted that boundaries were often violated, and jealous acrimony ensued when the partners used social media to connect with each other.

The ways of relating we currently experience in modern, everyday society, with its technological quick-fixes, have failed to provide us with an understanding of what could be going wrong in our intimate relations. We are becoming hardwired and quick to perceive all that is going right in the moment and ask questions about how to make it right, but we have lost the ability to carefully examine what could be wrong. Therefore, I titled the book "how not to fail," as opposed to "how to succeed," in order to take into account the current reality regarding rates of failure and the rapid advances and shifts in the forums used for communication.

As a psychotherapist, I have worked with individuals and couples for the last forty years, attempting to get people to understand the dynamics of what may be missing in their relationships as opposed to what is already good and existent. What is good and existent was never what brought people into treatment. Those aspects of what was missing or not working seemed to be what pained people more about their relationships, driving them to seek help.

What is missing from a relationship can often be elusive and seem intangible to the people in it. For the therapist, the problems can appear to be at an unconscious level, not available to the client to easily see and recognize. The often elusive, unseen aspects of their relationships usually had to do with what I term the "head, the heart, and the crotch" aspects of attachment. When I say "head, heart, crotch," I am referring to those separate functions that each possesses a life of their own in our individual psyche and how they affect our intimate relationships.

Why Psychotherapy Can Help

Psychotherapy is a treatment process that helps people identify, in themselves, the areas of internal mental functioning that are most problematic. It can also help them find conflict-free areas of functioning. This treatment attempts to resolve the everyday difficulties arising in people's lives. One actively looks at one's psycho-social self in an attempt to better understand why and how one copes with problems and how effectively one relates to other individuals.

Psychotherapists and psychoanalysts are trained to observe and study human behavior, primarily in three areas of human development: the brain, the heart, and the sexual/sensual development. The brain, the heart, and the sexual world of the individual are the domain of many forms of psychotherapy. This domain, coupled with the writings of moral philosophy that refer to the question of what is good and bad both in society and in human beings, are the cornerstones of modern-day psychology and psychotherapeutic treatment.

When I refer to "the brain" and "the heart," I am referring specifically to those mental processes—such as intellect and intelligence—which are associated with the brain, and one's affective world and feelings, commonly referred to as "the heart."

A trained therapist can look at the sexual functioning of his client to help the client understand whatever difficulties, fears, anxieties, taboos, inhibitions, or attachments the person may be experiencing in his intimate love relations. Again, this is what I mean when I speak of a "crotch" connection. The brain, the heart, and the sexual world of the individual are the domains examined in helping clients explore their relationships.

You may ask yourself, "Why are psychotherapists interested in these areas? How has psychology come to understand and focus on these areas of human functioning?" The answer may be found in an understanding of ancient Greek society and the beliefs of the Athenians. They emphasized that individual freedom and its ultimate expression was through the symmetry of body and mind. They believed that a fully developed human being was the individual who achieved the proper balance of spirit, mind, and body. The highly developed individual was the person who had worked on and came to the fullest realization and balance in these areas of their humanity.

When thinking of an appropriate twenty-first-century adaptation, I borrowed from the Greek concept and coined the phrase, "head, heart, crotch connection."

Unconscious Connections

Connections are often unconscious and driven by what we, first and foremost, are attracted to. Individuals project defined personas wishing to influence what others see and think of them, how they want others to perceive them, as well as how they choose to relate to others. It has been observed and written about in self-psychology that a person utilizes different aspects of "self" to interact with others:

- They can relate to the world through their head, projecting intellect or intelligence as their way of capturing the attention of others and engaging in the world.
- They can project emotionality, displaying their heartfelt feelings to others to engage and capture attention.
- They can attempt to engage with the world through their sexuality, displaying sexualized energy and sensuality to engage with others.

More challenging, yet most masterful and effective, would be to engage with others through a concerted use of the head, heart, and crotch—employing one's thoughts, feelings, and sensuality.

We, as individuals, are usually attracted to one or several aspects of the other person's projected persona, establishing initial connections to the most predominant projected image. We are unconsciously driven to connect with those imaged aspects and often have preferences for the type of person we relate to. Therefore, if we relate foremost to a person's intellect, we may tend to admire and seek thoughtful, bright, erudite individuals. If we relate to the emotional expressions of a person, we seek someone who exhibits their feelings foremost over their thoughts or sexuality. If we relate to a person's sexuality, first and foremost, we seek a person who exudes an attractive, sexualized image.

Identifying Your Connection Preference

For a person to understand their own head, heart, crotch connection, the challenge would be to identify what you relate to most, what you seek in others, and if there is an order or preference of interest. So, for example, do you first connect at the level of the head, the heart, the crotch, or any other combination of the three? Therefore, it requires you to identify your particular preference for connection and determine the order of your attraction.

An equally significant challenge would be determining how you project your imagined identity and whether it is with your head, your heart, or your sexuality. How people project themselves in their attempts to engage with the world underlies and defines their connections. In the subsequent chapters, we will dive deeper into these concepts.

CHAPTER 2

What is a Head Connection?

The head connection refers to what we as individuals think, conceive, believe, value, or esteem and how we project those thoughts onto our partners in a relationship. So, what we think can affect what our partners think or believe about us.

A head connection refers to our ability to say what is on our mind or expound on our thoughts and have them accepted by our partners in a gratifying way. So, for example:

- Do you respect and admire the things and ideas your partner speaks about?
- Does the way they express themselves make you feel pride, joy, satisfaction, or pleasure?
- Or do you find it difficult to relate to them, possibly feeling anger, annoyance, impatience, or perhaps revulsion?
- Do you find it difficult to make a connection to the thoughts, beliefs, or values they espouse?
- Are your thoughts and values similar or extremely disparate from your partner's?

- Where do you differ?
- Are these differences acceptable and tolerable, or do they cause you such conflict that they remain foreign and intolerable?

If our beliefs and thoughts are not pleasing to our partners, we will begin to reject them for what they believe or think. If what they think is unpleasing or offensive, we start to remove ourselves from them, not wanting to internalize or be associated with what and how they think. But, if we like their thought patterns, how they think, and what they believe, value, or say in expressing themselves, we begin to connect and attach to their way of thinking and experience "an identification" with their thoughts. This identification leads to bonding with them, resulting in the beginnings of a head connection.

Determine Shared Values vs. Conflicting Values

A person's ability to respect, admire and identify with the thoughts of the partner in a relationship sets the groundwork for a head connection. There should be a significant number of shared values in common and not a multitude of differences in values. This is not to imply that we will agree and respect all our partner's thoughts, beliefs, and values, but that there is enough pleasure experienced, not displeasure, to begin the process of connecting to their head. It should be respected where there is a difference and not result in ongoing acrimony. Your partner's ability to have you appreciate them for their values, thoughts, and beliefs will help to determine the success of your particular head connection.

You are probably questioning yourself right now and wondering what type of head connection you currently have with your partner, or equally important, if you are a head connection for your partner, and if it is a good one or if something is missing. Does your partner possess the qualities you look for in someone, or is the connection a weak one, lacking in strength and vitality or stimulation? You may be going so far as to question what it means if you don't have a good head connection.

CHAPTER 2

Does it necessarily mean that your relationship is over or that you are, perhaps, incompatible? The answer is "no," not necessarily, but you may have to consider how you will need to work on furthering a deeper head connection. It can be painstaking work to identify and admit to oneself that you may not be connecting to your partner intellectually or that you have avoided exploring it in an attempt to remain connected.

Examine Your Values

Determining your head connection requires self-reflection. Examining your values, beliefs, and thoughts and being truly honest with what you like or dislike in yourself and your partner is what it takes to recognize your head connection.

The word "values" implies your ideals, thoughts, standards, or morals. Knowing or remembering what you value in life is an effective way of helping you to cope with stressful situations. If you struggle with knowing your own values or beliefs, you will need to reflect on that to see if you share values with your partner or if your values conflict with theirs. A sort of value inventory is required to identify in yourself what you esteem, believe, and hold dear. Knowing your values can be particularly helpful when you find yourself troubled repeatedly by the same situations or with the same person.

Below is a list of possible values that influence thoughts, which could help determine the basis of your head connection.

- Loyalty
- Humility
- Compassion
- Honesty
- Integrity
- Kindness
- Altruism
- Selflessness

- Generosity
- Empathy

The Value of Empathy

Empathy, for example, can be identified in two ways:

1. Cognitive empathy describes the intellectual understanding of someone else's feelings without sensing them.
2. Affective empathy is feeling someone else's emotions as your own.

Do you or your partner possess either of these types of empathy sufficiently to encourage a positive head connection? Or do either of you (or both) lack empathy, which could keep one from connecting to a partner's values and beliefs?

For example, if you admire generosity and altruism, you might conclude that service to others is one of your cherished values. Moreover, you may decide that it is a value you look for in others and which most fosters a head connection for you.

Identification of values such as these are ways of exploring your beliefs and determining if you and or your partner either possess these attributes or if you struggle with them.

CHAPTER 2

Additional Resources to Explore Your Values

- For a fuller exploration of values, see the work of Nir Eyal, where he further explores the values we possess at https://www.nirandfar.com/common-values .[4]

- You can also learn more by visiting the MindTools Content Group at https://www.mindtools.com/a5eygum/what-are-your-values to determine your values and what is most important in life.[5]

- Discover your core values on Indeed by visiting https://www.indeed.com/career-advice/career-development/discover-core-values.[6]

- At the back of this book, see Appendix A: List of Common Values for a fuller example of values.

- For further exploration of value systems, consider taking the Valued Living Questionnaire developed by Kelly Wilson and Groom: https://div12.org/wp-content/uploads/2015/06/Valued-Living-Questionnaire.pdf.[7]

In the following chapters, I will address how to identify problems in head connections further after we explore what I refer to as heart and crotch connections.

---

4   Nir Eyal, "20 Common Values [and Why People Can't Agree on More]," Nir and Far, July 22, 2022, https://www.nirandfar.com/common-values/.
5   The Mind Tools Content Team By the Mind Tools Content Team et al., "What Are Your Values?: Deciding What's Most Important in Life," Decision-Making Skills from MindTools.com, accessed August 4, 2022, https://www.mindtools.com/pages/article/newTED_85.htm.
6   Indeed Editorial Team, "6 Steps to Discover Your Core Values," Indeed Career Guide, June 21, 2022.
7 Kelly Wilson and Groom, "Valued Living Questionnaire (VLQ) - div12. Org," Valued Living Questionnaire (VLQ), 2002.

CHAPTER 3

What Is a Heart Connection?

The heart aspect refers to how you feel, experience, treat, love, and sometimes even dislike aspects of your partner's emotional world or emotional expression towards you. The heart connection often gets us most confused when closely examining how we actually feel and how our partner feels emotionally towards us. The heart is what feels the wounds of betrayal and dissatisfaction and what informs the head that something is wrong, even if we can't always explain the anxiety associated with it.

Since the heart determines our affective states, when we ask ourselves if we feel truly happy with the emotions that our partner makes us feel, we get in touch with our genuine heart connection. If your partner displays concern and care in paying attention to how you feel, if they are gentle with and attentive to your feelings and careful not to abuse them, you will know what level of heart connection you may have. It is that ability of the person to know how you feel, guard those feelings and not shame them or abuse them in words or deeds that create a good heart connection. One's ability to acknowledge feelings, empathize, and express care for their partner's emotional world will help determine the success of your heart connection.

Six Basic Emotions

Emotions and feelings are often used interchangeably, but they are not the same thing. Emotions are considered to be subconscious and instinctive. People can have emotions internally without outwardly demonstrating them. Feelings are conscious. Feelings develop when your brain assigns a meaning to the emotion you are having.[8] Feelings are the outward expression of your emotions.

Psychologists Paul Ekman and Wallace Friesen have identified six basic emotions that all humans experience.[9] They have been identified as:

- happiness
- sadness
- disgust
- fear
- surprise
- anger

These basic emotions need to be identified in oneself and your partner's ability to recognize these in you. Although you may experience other emotions, if you feel that your relationship recognizes these basic emotions and can discuss or address them, this is the foundation for a good head connection.

---

[8] Betsy at Zen Mama et al., "What's the Difference between Feelings and Emotions?," The Best Brain Possible, June 17, 2021.

[9] Paul Ekman and Wallace Friesen, "Handbook of Cognition and Emotion," *Handbook of Cognition and Emotion*, February 25, 1999, pp. 45-57, https://doi.org/10.1002/0470013494.

CHAPTER 3

Identifying and Acknowledging Emotions

Beyond recognizing those basic emotions, it would be anticipated that your partner should be able to identify feeling states that are influenced by your emotions.

There are many more feeling states than there are emotions. Feelings such as:

Love	Joy
Hate	Ecstasy
Jealousy	Disappointment
Envy	Disillusionment
Kindness	Trust
Benevolence	Acceptance
Compassion	Respect
Empathy	Vulnerability

These are all examples of feelings that need to be acknowledged by you and your partner. It is of vital importance that you be able to distinguish between emotional and feeling states.

If you experience difficulty identifying a full range of feelings, see *The Dialectical Behavior Therapy Skills Workbook,* Chapter 3: Basic Mindfulness Skills List of Commonly Felt Emotions on page 75.[10]

At the back of this book, you can also see *Appendix B: List of Feelings Experienced* for a fuller list of feelings.

---

10   Matthew McKay Ph.D., Jeffrey C. Wood Psy.D., and Jeffrey Brantley MD, "DBT Skills Workbook - ADOECI," The Dialectical Behavior Therapy Skills Workbook (New Harbinger, 2007).

Intimacy

Intimacy is determined by the degree to which your partner is willing to work at recognizing feelings. As you examine different feeling states, you might want to explore each aspect of your relationship with your partner.

Questions you may wish to explore:

- Does the trust in your relationship involve feeling safe with allowing your partner to have insights about you that you normally would not confide with others?

- Does the relationship involve treating the other as if their thoughts and feelings are of value?

- Does the compassion displayed have a genuine concern for the issues that are concerning to you?

- Does the empathy shown demonstrate an ability to feel what the other person feels?

Again you may be questioning yourself right now and wondering what type of heart connection you currently have with your partner or if you are even compatible together.

I will address this possible concern later after we explore what the concept of a crotch connection symbolizes.

CHAPTER 4

What Is a Crotch Connection?

You could ask, "What is a crotch connection?"

When I say the crotch, it can refer to the actual physical anatomical organ and how excited or aroused we may be by viewing it. Still, even more broadly, it means the level of sexual energy, referred to as libido, that one has or exudes and how your partner in a relationship is experiencing it. For example, is the sexual energy displayed in the relationship pleasing and mutually gratifying, or is it experienced as an obligation one must perform to maintain the relationship?

I refer to the ability to sustain and experience pleasure and satisfaction, not emotional pain or aversion, in relating sexually to your partner as a crotch connection:

- When you are with your partner and that person is concerned about how you feel sexually.

- When they are concerned with providing you pleasure in addition to experiencing pleasure themselves, which results in orgasms for both partners.

This is what induces sexual intimacy and can lead to satisfaction. The degree of satisfaction depends on how sexually potent the relationship is and if both partners desire it. The ability to be concerned about the sexual well-being of your partner, their sexual needs, and whether or not they are feeling sexually pleased will determine the success of that connection.

In an article titled "Mutually Satisfying Sex in Your Marriage," Dr. Dave Currie and Glen Hoos note that in their clinical experience, they estimate that fewer than one-third of married couples they have treated enjoy a mutually satisfying sexual relationship.[11] They go on to explain that a married couple's sex life can not be fully gratifying if it is one-sided. One-sided sex produces resentment, not intimacy or closeness. Resentment can only lead to a sense of further disconnection.

So what does it take to create mutually gratifying sex and greater intimacy? It takes going beyond just recognizing or focusing on your sexual needs being met. It requires that we empathize with a partner's needs, attempt to see their perspective of what is gratifying, and have the willingness to work on meeting their needs. The act of empathy leads to greater attachment and furthers your sense of connection. Simply put, the lack of empathy creates disconnection. I do not portend that empathy alone is the cure-all for sexual satisfaction, but it is the linchpin to a better sexual connection.

In my opinion, the inability to experience cognitive or emotional empathy is the root of mutually ungratifying sexual experiences. The ability to empathize with your partner's sexual desires overcomes underlying difficulties such as lack of communication, self-consciousness, or feelings of unworthiness in relationships. When a partner can verbalize their concern for your sexual gratification, it serves to wither away many of the obstacles to mutually gratifying

---

[11] Dr. Dave Currie and Glen Hoos, "Mutually Satisfying Sex in Your Marriage," The Life, accessed August 31, 2022, https://thelife.com/mutual-satisfying-sex-in-your-marriage.

sex. When you verbalize your wish to satisfy and act upon it, it no longer serves as a reason for lack of gratification. Other problems may exist that affect sexual pleasure, but they are not based on an unwillingness or a one-sidedness of mutual gratification.

Noam Shpancer, Ph.D., in his Psychology Today article titled "Sexual Satisfaction: Highly Valued, Poorly Understood," notes that research shows "people in more intimate relationships, with good communication and mutual support, experience greater sexual satisfaction.[12] In the context of relationships, sexual assertiveness (the ability to stand your ground, establish clear boundaries, clarify what you want and need in sex, what works for you and what doesn't) predicts increased satisfaction."

But the demonstration of empathy is not the only factor influencing your connection. Among the barriers to mutually gratifying sexual experiences is the issue of safety in your connection. Do you feel safe to discuss sexual desires, free from self-shame or the fear of shame and ridicule from your partner (induced shame)? Mutually gratifying sex involves safety. Do you have a strong enough connection that allows you to express sexual desires, or do you feel shame discussing it or fear you will be shamed, or have you actually been shamed or ridiculed? If you do not feel safe in your ability to be yourself in a sexual relationship, you can not sustain a healthy connection. Healthy connections are expressed in the words that you ascribe to your experiences, such as pleasurable and mutual, among other sexual states of being. See Appendix C for a description of positive sexual expression.

Love (Attachment)

In his book, Healing the Shame That Binds You, John Bradshaw notes that "the power of the interpersonal bridge, along with a sense of identity, form the foundation for a healthy adult love

---

12 Noam Shpancer Ph.D., "Sexual Satisfaction: Highly Valued, Poorly Understood," Psychology Today (Sussex Publishers, February 16, 2014).

relationship.[13] A toxically shamed person is divided within himself and must create a false self-cover-up to hide his sense of being flawed and defective. You cannot offer yourself to another person if you do not know who you are."

Bradshaw explores how shame-based affects (feelings) keep us from experiencing our authentic selves. Toxic shame inhibits and binds us from seeking sexual connection or from feeling attached once involved in a relationship. He states that by "having a secure attachment with one's original parental figures, and having developed a sense of worth, a person feels he is lovable and wants to love another. A securely attached person with a solid sense of self is capable of connecting with another in an intimate relationship. Intimacy requires vulnerability and a lack of defensiveness. Intimacy requires healthy shame." Toxic shame, internalized and experienced as unsafe, keeps us from experiencing our true uninhibited sexual self. But feeling safe allows for vulnerability and freedom of expression of our sexual wishes.

The demonstration of concern over the sexual well-being of your partner, their sexual needs, your sexual needs, the feeling of mutuality, your personal sense of identity, and whether or not you feel safe in the encounter helps determine the success of your crotch connection.

How you connect intellectually, emotionally, and sexually can be based on your attachment style. The British psychologist, John Bowlby, wrote in the '60s about three types of attachment styles: secure, avoidant, and anxious-ambivalent. Bowlby notes that as we grow up, through interactions with significant others, we internalize a specific "attachment style" to relate to the world and the person in it.

A specific attachment style can shape a child's emotional response patterns and interpersonal behaviors way into adulthood. If your adult sexuality is defined by any one of these attachment styles, it has implications for your connections:

---

[13] John Bradshaw, "Healing the Shame That Binds You," John Bradshaw, October 15, 2005, https://www.johnbradshaw.com/books/healing-the-shame-that-binds-you.

1. Secure attachment: the world is safe and trusting, needs will be met, and people are trustworthy.

2. Avoidant attachment: the world is unsafe, people are not helpful, self-reliance is needed, and avoidance of people is necessary.

3. Anxious-ambivalent attachment: people are to be feared; they may hurt you; I want closeness but fear others will not offer intimacy or closeness.

These all have implications for connection. Sexuality approached from an avoidant or anxious-ambivalent attachment style will clearly result in some level of disconnection. On the other hand, a secure attachment style clearly can lead to a closer connection. Shpancer notes that research done at the University of Waterloo in Canada by researchers E. Sandra Byers and Uzma S. Rehman demonstrated that a secure attachment style was predictive of increased sexual satisfaction.[14]

The question of how much sexual gratification is needed is one we all grapple with, especially early in the relationship. The quantity and quality of sexual intimacy at the beginning of a relationship can sometimes overshadow the need for intellectual and emotional gratification. But as the relationship progresses, we become more keenly aware of what is occurring outside the bedroom, in the head and heart realm of the relationship. In my experience, this is a fairly normal progression and can be anticipated if one hopes to attain the fullest head, heart, crotch connection.

Overcoming Obstacles

If you are experiencing difficulty obtaining mutually gratifying sexual experiences or suffering from shame-based affects, I would suggest you consider the following steps to help overcome these obstacles:

- Speak with your partner about any fear or shame experienced.

---

14   E. Sandra Byers and Uzma Rehman, "Sexual Well-Being | Request PDF - Researchgate," January 2014, https://www.researchgate.net/publication/290485042_Sexual_well-being.

- Discuss what mutually gratifying sex may mean to both of you.
- Look for educational material on sexuality in general and specifically on shame.
- Consider seeking professional help via a certified, licensed sex therapist.

Resources you may want to consider include books like John Bradshaw's Healing the Shame that Binds You to address possible shame-based feelings and The Joy of Sex by Alex Comfort, Ph.D., to explore sexuality and the concept of mutuality.

In these preceding chapters, I artificially separated each connection into distinct categories but will again integrate them into a unified concept demonstrating how and when the three come together. I will describe how head, heart, and crotch connections influence our attachments and how one explores and interprets the connections at the level of head, heart, and crotch, understanding their importance to the successful outcome of your relationship. It is what I will label as the 6 W's of connection and why words matter.

CHAPTER 5

Words Create Experience

Clearly, my work with clients guided my thinking and helped me formulate interventions around the connections made to the head, heart, and crotch. It helped me see how exploring these connections my clients made in their relationships was vital in getting them to see how they were relating to their partners and if there was something perhaps missing in one of the areas that needed addressing. I thought it necessary to explore various questions regarding the nature of connections.

Questions such as the "who," "why," "what," "which," "where," and "when" of connections became paramount in understanding how head, heart, crotch connections occur.

The 6 W's of Connection: Who, Why, What, Which, Where, and When

The questions I posed to my clients were:

> Who is the type of person you are most attracted to?
>
> Why do you find the connection attractive?

> What is the order of your attraction?
>
> Which type of connection is most important to you?
>
> Where does your strongest connection lie?
>
> When does a connection fail?

As a therapist, the questions I had to explore to determine the outcome of a connection were:

> When does overlooking or underestimating the value of a connection have implications for a relationship?
>
> When and why can you fail to recognize the significance of a particular connection?
>
> Which connection could possibly compensate for the lack of another?

I assumed that by objectively exploring the true nature of one's intimate connections to the mind, heart, and body, one begins to evaluate the faults and strengths in the relationship and whether or not to work on and improve those connections. I believe that improvements in each of your connections to the mind, heart, and body create and release attachment bonds. As I convinced clients to more clearly differentiate between the connections made to the head, heart, and crotch and to verbalize the who, what, where, when, which, and why of their thoughts and feelings regarding their connections, they were then able to see if their attachments were secure or insecure.

Discussing the Head, Heart, Crotch Connection

When my clients were able to say what they liked and disliked about their mind connection, what they liked and disliked about their heart connection, and what they liked and disliked about their sexual connection, then they were able to move on with becoming more intimate. If the attachment felt too disconnected, they could decide to entertain the idea of the dissolution of their relationship. The hope was that the relationship would benefit from this level of analysis, but if exploration resulted in the ending of a failing unsatisfactory relationship, that was of equal value as well.

When I first introduced the idea that relationships could be described in terms of their connectedness to the head, heart, and crotch, my clients would often glance at me strangely, appearing doubtful, as if they were looking at a two-headed llama. I would go on to explain that this area of pursuit was perhaps new to them and that it might feel like I was peering into their deepest-held secrets. They would often react with anxious, sheepish laughter or turn away. Others reacted offensively and would frown inquisitively as if I were in some way a peeping tom looking into their souls. It could be off-putting for some, usually depending on their socialization, background, or how they were raised.

I noticed that my female clients were often more at ease discussing their head and heart connection but, admittedly, were not used to discussing their crotch connection in those terms. Many male clients appeared to be socialized to speak of their libidinal wishes and desires more readily, as well as their connection to sexual body parts. As I explored further and gave permission to talk about sexual wishes, desires, and fantasies, most clients felt freer to explore their connections.

At first, they would explain their problems with limited employment of words in vague terms. Clients would say, "I like his head because he is intelligent and funny and his heart because he is kind."

Putting Words to Experience

I often found myself getting them to expound on their verbal descriptions of their thoughts and feelings to establish a deeper understanding of their connections. I would tell my clients that, much like the Aleutians who have over one hundred words to describe snow, I needed to get them to expand their use of words to explain their head and heart connection. To describe their head connection, I would offer them an array of descriptive words such as:

Head, Heart, Crotch Connections

Bright
Verbal
Sophisticated
Curious
Flexible
Unbiased

Impartial
Rational
Objective
Thoughtful
Honest

However, a negative mindset was connotated by words such as:

Dull
Naïve
Sullen
Gloomy
Unsophisticated
Ignorant
Valueless
Devaluing
Close-minded
Stubborn
Rigid
Inflexible

Prejudicial
Judgmental
Irrational
Subjective
Opinionated
Cynical
Sarcastic
Duplicitous
Deceptive
Cunning
Manipulative

When provided with an array of words that better described possible thoughts and emotions, my clients were somehow empowered to acknowledge their experiences to characterize their connections better. As you narrate your story and put words to your experiences, you can either increase or decrease the quality of your connection.

CHAPTER 5

Dr. Brené Brown, the famous clinical social-work author, and inspirational speaker, in her most recent book, Atlas of the Heart, refers to a saying by Ludwig Wittgenstein: "the limits of my language means the limits of my world."[15] She was referring to the twentieth century philosopher Ludwig Wittgenstein's belief about language and the use of words. The statement refers to the belief that if one cannot describe something in words, then it perhaps does not exist. Brene Brown's goal in her book is to help individuals expand the language they employ to communicate their feelings and build an emotional vocabulary.[16] Dr. Brené Brown notes that "language is a portal that transports us to a universe of new choices and second chances—a universe where we can share the stories of our bravest and most heartbreaking moments with each other in a way that builds connection."[17]

Experiences Create Attachment

Words create our experiences; they ascribe meaning to our lived encounters—the use of words fully elaborate experience. When we think about our experiences, we use words to enrich them. The more nuanced and descriptive the words one can employ to describe our thoughts and feelings, the more we create bonds of attachment to the experiences. An embellished experience creates deeper bonds of attachment. In turn, the more intense the bond, the stronger the connection.

Using a paucity of words to describe our thoughts and feelings leads to a weaker bonding to those experiences, which results in a lesser intense connection.

---

15   Brown Brené and Gavin Aung Than, Atlas of the Heart: Mapping Meaningful Connection and the Language of Human Experience (New York, NY: Random House Large Print, 2021).
16   Oprah and Brené Brown on "Cultivating Connection," Oprah Daily, November 28,2021. Retrieved Dec 30, 2021.
17   Brown Brené and Gavin Aung Than, Atlas of the Heart: Mapping Meaningful Connection and the Language of Human Experience (New York, NY: Random House Large Print, 2021).

Therefore, in therapy with my clients, I never allowed for vague descriptions of experiences that never fully described their connections. Instead, I would always encourage them to be as specific as possible to propel bonding experiences and further enhance connections.

Asking clients to determine if they believe, value, respect, or appreciate what their partners think, voice, or espouse was not always easily achieved. It was more familiar to get them to say if they appreciate their partner's emotional treatment of them. More often than not, they would say that no one has ever asked them to describe these concerns. I would say that a good therapist gets their client to express their genuine thoughts and feelings fully without limitation, vagueness, or inhibition. The more in touch you are with exactly what you think and feel, the more intense the sense of attachment or connection to the other.

Most baffling to clients was trying to get them to say what their partner's connection to them may have been.

What did their partner admire, love, or dislike about them?

What did they believe was their partner's mental, emotional, and sexual connection to them?

Exploring this was often more painstaking than describing their connection to their partner. Exploring their partner's connection to them felt scary, uncharted, sometimes indescribable, and inevitably fraught with anxiety at the thought that their partner may not be as connected as they had imagined. Fears of abandonment and disconnect often surfaced when asked to consider their partner's connection to them, appearing inexpressible or unutterable. Clients would express feeling more vulnerable than when talking about their own sense of connection.

Relating to the Full Person

One of the major problems that would arise is that clients would often speak about relating to parts of the person but not to the full person. You have to ask yourself what and how you are relating to

CHAPTER 5

your partner. Do you love or relate to all aspects of their being, their head, heart, and crotch, or are you just relating to parts of them?

What do I mean by this? It's like a patchwork or the pieces of a puzzle. Are you picking and choosing the parts you relate to? Are you building a patchwork of connections, or is it like a puzzle where you connect the pieces that do not fully connect?

CHAPTER 6

The Head, Heart, Crotch Connection Is Like a Puzzle

When I say that head, heart, crotch connections are like a puzzle, it's because puzzles are a game we enjoy; we like to put together the missing parts into a whole picture. What happens when we are unable to bring the picture together, or there is a missing part of a puzzle? It leads to confusion and a sense of dissatisfaction or emptiness. This emptiness becomes more noticeable as we observe the puzzle and see that things are missing. What is missing becomes ever more glaring and noticeable, making us yearn for completion and satisfaction.

When we experience a missing part of the head, heart, crotch connection, we yearn for completeness and a fuller connection. When we don't have it or become aware of how a piece may be missing, we begin to either fight for it or lose interest and give up being able to attain it. How this happens depends upon our own ability to satisfy our fantasies about the person we are relating to, as well as how our relationships with significant loved ones in our life helped us sustain intimacy. When we, as children, related to our family, specifically our parents, we often invested much energy in relating to them. When we received much of the emotional love and nurturance we needed, we learned that our dependency needs could be met fairly quickly or deeply. This led to an ability to look for our needs being met through an intense "relating to" our loved ones.

What happens when our dependency and attachment needs are not satisfied or met by our loved ones? When our parents were too busy, unable, or unwilling to meet our needs and gratify our wishes to whatever degree, we became frustrated with them and their inability or unwillingness to be there for us. What did we do? We could have become demanding and clinging, as children often do when their needs are not met, or we could have turned away in disappointment and frustration as some children do.

In this turning away and its resultant sense of disappointment lies the root of our subsequent reactions as adults when our adult partners do not meet our dependency/intimacy needs. We begin to relate to them as we did as children to our parents. We can become angry or frustrated and demanding, or we can turn away in frustration and look elsewhere for our needs to be met. We no longer find ourselves idealizing our significant other; instead, we begin to devalue them.

Polar Opposite

When the idealization of the other begins to fail us, we can often swing to the other polar opposite side and employ devaluing reactions. But in order to maintain a healthy connection, we need to see how we employ idealizing and devaluing views while exploring our unmet childhood dependency needs through a realistic examination of who and what our partners represent for us. Devaluation brought on by unmet dependency needs can result in rejection of the other.

In turning away from our loved ones, we begin to fantasize that our needs can never be met or possibly be met elsewhere. It is the start of a psychic detachment that can lead to the demise of a relationship.

CHAPTER 6

In the chapter on what affects success, I will examine more the idea of fantasy bonds and how our relationships are affected by re-enactments of childhood interactions. But the following chapter will focus on why a relationship can fail.

CHAPTER 7

Why a Relationship Can Fail

How do we start to move away emotionally, intellectually, and physically? Why and how does that demise happen? When do we begin to lose it for our partners?

We can start by noticing how our significant other is not as bright as we originally thought or how they think is really not as connected to our way of thinking. We begin to feel a sense of disconnect from them, and we can then begin to devalue them for it, as opposed to respecting the differentness and uniqueness from our way of thinking. Their way of thinking becomes repugnant to us at some level rather than an attractive aspect of them.

Demise of the Head Connection

Of course, this often occurs at an unconscious or subconscious level over time, and when we initially sense it, we can either start to fight it off by complaining to our partners or begin distancing ourselves through disinterest and lack of communication. Again, the choice of reaction is often influenced by how we reacted as children to how our parents thought. Did we always admire our parents for their thoughts, or did we turn away from their way of thinking? Did we fight with them as we often do during our adolescence, or did we identify and totally relate to them, taking in wholeheartedly what they thought, not to be challenged in any way?

As adults, we learn to relate to our current partners in much the same way we did with our parents, or we have unconscious desires to swing the other way and not to relate to them as we may have done with our parents. Either choice we made as children affects what we do as adults with our current partners.

It would be nice to say that the manner of relating to our current partners is always in our control, but often it is not. It is often driven by unconscious or subconscious elements of our psyche. However, when it becomes conscious, we are in a better position to challenge our feelings and sustain our intimacy rather than becoming disappointed and distancing ourselves or getting angry and fighting with our partners over our sense of dissatisfaction with them. Either position we hold can influence the eventual outcome.

We can either voice our dissatisfaction and hope that our partner can change and achieve a sense of resolution, or we can turn away, remaining angry and unfulfilled. This is often the case when a relationship starts to dissolve, and the person is unable to remain connected out of their own sense of overwhelming disappointment, frustration, and resulting detachment. They begin to move away head-wise from their purported loved one. This is how a head connection can lose its attachment and become devalued and disconnected.

Demise of the Heart Connection

So what occurs in the area of the heart, and how does that connection happen? We are most vulnerable to losing a heart connection based on how our partners treat us emotionally and how reminiscent it was or was not of our parents. When we come from parents who emotionally care for us, meaning they do not abandon us, neglect us, or abuse us, we learn to feel safe and satisfied with that type of love. A love that is kind, gentle, careful, and respectful of our feelings is a form of love that is internalized and wants to be relived in all our adult relations.

An emotional love that is cruel, harsh, rough, and conditional is a form of love that results in our identifying with hostility, manipulation, and aggression. We learn that is what love consists of, and we seek that form of love rather than an unconditional, respectful, warm, caring form of love. If we did not receive a healthy form of love as children, we do not know what healthy love looks like. When it does come our way, we are distrustful of it and can abandon it out of fear. It is foreign to us, and we are uncomfortable with it, not knowing what it and its parameters are. We distrust those who love unconditionally and wholeheartedly, but unconsciously we yearn for it.

The tragedy is that when we have not been loved as children, we don't really know what love is. We fantasize about love, but when true love comes, it can be so foreign that we can't tolerate its differentness or strangeness. We can become fearful and paranoid of it and then, in turn, reject it as not being true love.

Herein lies the confusion: the missing piece of the puzzle. We can not live without the missing piece but are so frightened of losing it that we'd rather reject it than take a chance of losing it or it leaving us. When the fears of our emotional needs and dependency wishes are not understood, we can often run away from our partners out of our own inability to tolerate frustration. Or we run away, either out of our own sadness and feelings as if we will never be loved the way we think we need to be, or in anger that our partners will never meet our wishes.

We can become either angry and demanding of emotional understanding, or we can become saddened and disappointed, not fighting *for* them, and then emotionally distance ourselves. Unfortunately, either reaction often results in the demise of the heart connection.

Demise of the Crotch Connection

What happens in the sexual arena? How does a sexual-crotch connection occur, and how do we sustain or lose it?

Head, Heart, Crotch Connections

Is sexual connection related to performance, size, physical attributes, or another strange form of chemistry? This is perhaps not as easily understood as the head and heart connection. For some, it may have nothing to do with the attributes before mentioned, and yet for others who are more keenly focused on sexual prowess, it may have everything to do with the aforementioned attributes. But the one area of crotch connection that is prone to disconnection has to do with the ability of the partner to make their beloved feel safe and wanted or desired.

A crotch connection can be physical, but more often than not, it is sensual:

- Can your partner please you through their actions and concern for your sexual satisfaction?
- Does your partner wish to satisfy themselves and not concern themselves with your satisfaction?
- Are they willing to satisfy you while satisfying themselves, or does it become a sexual war of pleasure and satisfaction?

A crotch connection that results in sexual satisfaction is one in which there is mutual satisfaction and concern for each other's gratification. When one partner is only concerned about their own gratification and not about pleasing and gratifying their partner, dissatisfaction begins, and potential fantasy and a wish for a different partner arises.

You could ask yourself, "How does the crotch connection sustain itself?" or "How does it lose its valence and intensity?" A crotch connection can and will depend not only on how sexual the partner is but also on how sexually interested the partner remains throughout the relationship. If your partner feels dissatisfied and there is a missing piece to the sexual connection, it can result in anger and frustration, either voiced or unvoiced, and a resulting desire to be with someone else, or it can lead to sexual distancing and fantasying about being with others. When the sexual desire is experienced as anger and frustration, it can lead to aggressive sexual connections or outright disparaging of the partner.

CHAPTER 7

Sexual frustration experienced as unwillingness to please the other becomes part of the intimate relating and can have destructive effects on the relationship. That is the case within relatively healthy relationships, which are not characterized by sadomasochistic elements. It is not within the purview of this book to focus on aggressive sadomasochistic sexual relationships, so I will speak only of relationships that do not contain overtly sadomasochistic aspects to them.

When sexual feelings are left unsatisfied, and the person does not allow themselves to experience anger or frustration, the alternate reaction can be to remain silent, internalizing their frustration, and becoming sexually distant or removed and apparently disinterested. This can lead to a wish to be with someone else who would satisfy you sexually or an increase in fantasies about it. But, again, either reaction can lead to the demise of a crotch connection.

CHAPTER 8

The Importance of a Head, Heart, Crotch Connection

You could be asking yourself, "Why should I concern myself with whether or not I have a head, heart, crotch connection, and what is so important about it?" Determining whether or not you have healthy connections within these three areas of your interpersonal life can help you determine how genuinely happy you are in your relationship and, more importantly, can lead to your maintaining loving, intimate relatedness.

When relationships work, they are bound by an attraction that is usually unconscious but can often be understood if we take the time to think about where we stand regarding these three areas of our life. Granted, the conscious thinking of these three areas is hard work, and we can often overlook them as not being essential or important to maintaining the relationship. However, when a relationship starts to go awry, there actually are determinants and reasons for its often slow, unperceived demise.

When a relationship begins to fail, there were unperceived signs, writings on the wall, so the speak, which we overlooked or were too afraid to address had we only taken the time to consider our connection of the head, the heart, and crotch, as well as our partner's head, heart, crotch connection to us. Doing the work would place us in a better position to recognize where we stand in our current intimate relatedness: if it can be improved, how it can be the cause of our dissatisfaction, and how our relationship could fail. An ounce of prevention is worth a pound of cure.

Addressing Missing Pieces

What can you do if, after looking at your head, heart, crotch connection, you notice something is missing or has gone awry? Can it be fixed? Can you address it, or should you just learn to live with it and be satisfied with what already exists?

All fair yet difficult issues to consider.

When one comes to terms with what is missing in their relationship, it is often perceived as too late, or one has lost the willingness to do something about it. Or becoming aware of what is missing can lead you down a journey of trying to either fix it or down a different path of looking elsewhere.

Fixing it implies trying to either change the other person or change oneself and one's desires or expectations. One has to ask oneself, are my expectations reasonable, or are they totally unreasonable and could never be fulfilled by even the most intimately relatable partner? Sometimes our needs for admiration, love, and dependence are so huge that no one person could possibly meet them. Then one would have to question, "What is going on that would require such insatiable supplies of love and gratification? Did I not get enough unconditional parental love that I now want my current love object to provide for everything I did not get in my childhood?"

This type of inquiry could result in your saying that "maybe it is me that has the problem" as opposed to "my partner" or "the relationship." When demands for love are so overwhelming and time-consuming, one would need to question the individual's emotional state and if they can handle the normal demands of an

CHAPTER 8

interpersonal relationship. But if there are some areas of frustration and unfulfillment in your relationship that you perceive as not overwhelming or impossible to fulfill, it would behoove you to try to work on the missing pieces of the puzzle.

"Why?" you ask. Because there is no perfect relationship or perfect head, heart, crotch connection; all connections at some level will be left wanting or needing for more, and it is up to you to determine where and when each connection works or doesn't work and what would be needed to make it work. Bottom line: it's work.

Appreciating the Value of Connection

Does overlooking or underestimating the value of a connection have implications for a relationship? Can you fail to recognize the significance of a particular connection? Can satisfaction in one connection compensate for the lack of another?

In my clinical practice, I recall the case of a young, 30-year-old female client who sought treatment because she had a partner of ten years whom she began to perceive as "not terribly exciting." He had been more so when they first met, as evidenced by his wish to go out dancing, go on vacations, and explore sports. During the beginning of their relationship, she perceived him as fun-loving, exciting, and adventurous and described a fairly healthy love life. However, as the relationship progressed, he became less and less interested in emotional expressions of love and the activities that gave her pleasure. In addition, she claimed that he worked harder and harder at his job and became more concerned with his business ideas, political leanings, and beliefs.

I explored with her the initial connections she expressed having had for him. She mentioned having had a strong heart and crotch connection and also felt she had a fairly good head connection to her partner since she admired his intelligence. Within a few years of marriage and his experiencing a decreased interest in socializing and partaking in social activities, she began to feel bored and think of him as no longer fun-loving, adventurous, exciting, or in love with her.

Head, Heart, Crotch Connections

She expressed these feelings to him over time, but he didn't pick up on her concern or attempt to change. She admits to a continued dissatisfaction with him regarding how she felt about him emotionally. She acknowledged that she started to devalue him in her mind and think of him as not able or unwilling to change. Determined not to lose out on her past strivings, she started calling friends and going out to clubs. She said she had always enjoyed dancing and wanted to relive that experience again. She met an old friend she knew from years ago, from her college days, who reminded her of their shared interests. She started going out with him more regularly until she became emotionally attached to the fun-loving spirit she thought he possessed.

An affair started with this gentleman out of what she described as her need to fill the emotional void she was experiencing. The relationship eventually became sexual, and she claimed she accidentally came down pregnant. She had the child and never informed her husband of the child's paternity.

Several years into the ongoing affair, the gentleman wanted to get to know his son. My client was, at that point, unwilling to accept him meeting his son since he had not been in her son's life. Angered by her refusal, he posted videos of their affair on social media. This created shame for her, induced sadness, and an immediate withdrawal and disconnect from him.

My client was frightened by his demands and, feeling exposed by the revelations, came to seek therapy. She acknowledged how her initial connection with her husband started, how her attachment changed, and how they grew apart the more she devalued the emotional connection to him. She was able to acknowledge having had a "heart, crotch, head" connection to her husband but that her heart connection waned over time. She started to look for a replacement for the emotional connection she once had with her husband through an extramarital affair.

Once she discovered that the affair was no longer emotionally gratifying, she attempted to re-establish a connection she thought she once possessed with her husband. Feeling betrayed, her husband was initially enraged when he was informed of the affair and the child's existence but subsequently chose to forgive her. He was able to admit that he had emotionally abandoned her in the relationship and that this may have led to her looking outside of the marriage for a different heart connection. His willingness to forgive her for the mistake in judgment allowed her to return to the marriage with a renewed wish for connection.

When asked about her connection with her husband, she voiced feeling that it had changed in order of attachment from "heart, crotch, head" to becoming a "head, heart, crotch" connection. She realized that mentally, his intellect and values, as well as his emotional kindness and forgiving nature, are what saved their marriage and what she most loved. His mind and heart had overshadowed and taken precedence over the physical/sexual aspect of the relationship. Nonetheless, she felt she had achieved a head, heart, crotch connection that was fulfilling to her. She felt she was happy with her newfound mind, spirit, body connection.

CHAPTER 9

What Affects Success?

How do we handle frustration? Is frustration handled with a fight or flight response? When angered or frustrated, do you become visibly angry, or do you run away? Is your instinct one of fight, or is it one of flight? The degree to which you can address this issue in your behavior will have implications for success in your relationship.

Can you manage your anger, which is really just a cover-up, a disguise for your feelings of sadness? Can you talk about your sadness and disappointments about your partner, or do you run and hide and deny that they exist or wish they would just go away? As opposed to yelling and screaming, can you let your partner know your sadness and disappointment in them? Do you run away from confrontation in fear and anguish like when you were a child? Do you run away but then come back emboldened and want to talk? Do you create emotional distance by accusing your partner of being like others from your past? Do you run away to the consoling arms of a fantasied partner who will rescue you from your failing relationship?

Where Fantasy and Flight Works but for a While

When we choose the flight response as part of our behavior, we choose to let go of the fight, or in essence, our anger, in favor of an escape—an escape from intimacy. We fantasize that there is someone out there who will be able to satisfy our every need—someone who will be a better head, heart, crotch connection, the perfect friend, companion, partner, and lover, failing to realize that no such thing exists, yet caught up in the childhood fantasy that our perfect mate will be out there and rescue us from unfulfilling love. True, there may be someone out there better suited to fulfill your needs, but will you be able to perceive that fully and without guilt or shame if you have not resolved or understood your current relationship?

In his article, "The Fantasy Bond: A substitute for a truly loving relationship," Dr. Robert Firestone explains how most people have fears of intimacy, become self-protective, and are terrified of being alone.[18] Their response to these issues is to form fantasy bonds. He states that "this illusion of connection and closeness allows them to maintain an imagination of love and loving while preserving emotional distance. Destructive fantasy bonds, which exists in a large majority of relationships, greatly reduce the possibility of couples achieving intimacy."

He goes on to describe the fantasy bond as a compulsion to relive the past within our current relationships—a wish to form fantasized connections that unfailingly lead to reenacting interpersonal behaviors developed in childhood. A fantasy bond is a way of connecting to a person not based on who they actually are, but on our need to re-enact childhood conflicts originally formed with our parents to gain a sense of mastery and security in the present. We recreate the interactions that we know and are comfortable with from our past childhood encounters.

A fantasy bond is the result of emotional pain from childhood. When our parents are unable to provide the love we need, children form an illusion of being loved and united with the parent to

---

18   Ph.D Robert Firestone, "The Fantasy Bond: A Substitute for a Truly Loving Relationship," PsychAlive, October 4, 2016.

substitute for what was absent. The more deprived the child, the more the fantasy can be created. The child may begin to believe that they need no one other than themselves or that no one can meet their needs. Later, as adults, they can reject closeness out of fear of fulfilling unmet needs and dread of abandonment. They become reluctant to take a chance on intimate attachments.

Childhood defenses and childhood reactions being re-enacted can damage adult relationships. If in our childhood, we were not able to tolerate frustration, anger, or sadness, and if we ran in fear of our emotions, we can and often will re-enact these behaviors in the present. These difficulties are brought into our current relationships by those unresolved conflicts from our past.

The beginning of a relationship is often characterized by merging with the other in an attempt to create closeness. With time we can often lose our separateness as two to become one. But in this merging to become like one, we can begin to fear our closeness and move away emotionally, intellectually, and sexually. A fantasy bond originates in a fear of loss or abandonment and results in fleeing from emotional intimacy as soon as closeness develops.

Fantasy bonds occur when we see others not for who they really are but for who we wish them to be, often based on a childhood wish to recreate our family relationships with our current partners in the present to establish a sense of safety and security. But this sense of security becomes threatened as we become more intimate, experience differentness from the other, and begin to question our connection. In a fantasy bond, an intimate connection can change from being two independent persons in love to being two dependent people. Once this type of merging begins, conflict can ensue once there is a turn towards differentness, towards separation-individuation. Individual emotional freedom is no longer valued and is replaced by control or dominance in the relationships. Disconnection begins when the other is no longer seen as a separate individual with thoughts, feelings, and sexual desires different from one's own.

Importance of Separateness

Lisa Firestone, Ph.D., notes that once a person forms the illusion of being together as one, they begin to lose the sense of being together as two.[19] Accordingly, she states, "these behaviors deny the innate separateness of two individuals in a relationship, yet at the same time, they create a real distance by breeding resentment and a desire to be free from the roles and restrictions imposed by a forced sense of connection." She notes that we should be wary of times when we no longer relate to our partners as the person they may be but are purely making a connection to sustain our own sense of security.

A fantasy bond can work for a while since it acts to make a person feel as if they are a unit, a whole. But as the relationship progresses, the individual no longer feels free to express their real feelings and desires, losing their own distinctive points of view and opinions, inhibiting themselves within the relationship. Here is where disconnection can originate and where fantasy only works for a while. A fantasy bond is actually an escape from connection. It is the antithesis of a healthy connection where you feel free to express your feelings and have the other respect them. A relationship in which you have become like one, which does not allow for separateness or the expression and respect of each other's intellect, emotions, and sexual desires, is based on suppression of self and an unconscious wishful bonding fantasy.

Overcoming and avoiding fantasy bonds is a key element in creating greater connection. Acceptance of difference and separateness of your thoughts and feelings from those of others can be what most influences and affects success in a head, heart, crotch connection.

If you wish to learn more about the effects of fantasy bonds on relationships, I suggest you see https://www.psychalive.org/ the- fantasy- bond- substitute- for- a-loving relationship/.

---

19 PsychAlive, "Fantasy Bond," PsychAlive, February 25, 2021, https:// www.psychalive.org/fantasy-bond/.

CHAPTER 10

When and How to Address Your Current Head, Heart, Crotch Connection

Addressing the fledging and failing aspects of one's relationship can be scary and very difficult for most individuals. Nevertheless, it has to be done to sustain a good, working, loving relationship.

Can you be honest with yourself about the level of attachment you have with your partner concerning connection to mind, body, and spirit? If there is a missing piece, does it mean that the relationship is failed to doom? Or can you intervene in some way to prevent failure?

The Head Connection: Respect and Admiration

Experience has shown me that when an individual explores the nature of their connection, they often gain new levels of insight into the relationship that did not exist previously. Looking at how you relate to your partner's way of thinking can be satisfying if and when you come away saying that, on many issues, you admire their way of thinking, their beliefs, and how they express themselves is usually pleasing to you. If not, you would need to be able to verbalize to your partner how, when, and if what they voice and say offends you, rubs you the wrong way, or outright angers or annoys you, and be prepared to say why.

The "why" part has much to do with how "in touch" you are with your own beliefs, values, standards, and morals. You may not be able to change your partner's personal values necessarily, but you may be able to affect them by changing what they know about your beliefs. They would need to know that they stand on shaky ground if they continue to affront your beliefs and that it could lead to a distancing between you. It takes maturity and insight to perceive how clashes and acrimony within the mental sphere can drive people apart instead of bringing them closer together. That is not to say that couples cannot have differences in the way they think, but it is how they express those differences and the level of respect for one's partner's ability to tolerate those differences that needs to be understood.

If differences can be voiced in a respectful, kind manner and the difference doesn't become a continuous point of contention between you, then the difference can be tolerated, and a devaluing of the other may not occur. Instead of devaluing, respect and admiration occur despite the apparent differences.

The Heart Connection: Empathy and Sensitivity

The heart connection requires a deeper understanding of empathy and sensitivity to others. The ability to put yourself in the other person's shoes and be open and sensitive to their feelings is required in relationships. What and how another may feel is not always easily perceived, but the ability to empathize, or the lack thereof, will often determine the success of the heart connection.

Treating the other as you wish to be treated, spoken to, and felt by is always safe. Relationships that have lost the ability to empathize are often ones in which one of the partners is overly self-centered, self-absorbed, indifferent or hostile, and downright cruel. A person who does not care or think about how their partner feels cannot emotionally meet them in a loving place.

Questions that need to be asked about the head, heart, crotch issues are:

1. Does my partner respect and admire my thoughts?
2. Does my partner appreciate my emotions, empathize with my feelings, and consider my feelings?
3. Does my partner share equally in their sexual pleasure, showing concern for my satisfaction, as well as theirs?

Having a partner who respects your thoughts, way of thinking, and expressed points of view can be very rewarding intellectually. A partner who makes you feel like you are bright, creative, intelligent worthy of being listened to and respected reaches the part of your brain which stimulates further thought and a desire to continue to share your thoughts.

In contrast, a person who doesn't respect your thoughts will attempt to tear you down, make you feel unintelligent and worthless, or can further inhibit you or cause you to repress your thoughts out of fear or shame that what you think is not worthwhile. Alternatively, are those individuals who will attempt to gain respect by fighting for it with their thoughts and arguing points of view to gain respect.

Danger Signs

In the long haul, having to fight or argue to gain respect can and will wear a person down to the point where they eventually give up and turn elsewhere to share their thoughts with someone who will listen keenly to them. Here belies the first danger sign of turning away from your relationship and looking outwards:

> When you begin to think that someone else finds you more intellectually stimulating than your partner or when you see your partner as no longer intellectually engaging, you may start sharing your thoughts with others in an attempt

to gain the desired thoughtful head connection you do not possess or have lost with your partner.

Many relationships have started in the workplace or schools of learning, for example, because of an intellectual connection that one may feel towards another individual, regardless of how else the relatedness may be or fail to be. The mind is a very powerful prevailing feature of a person's relatedness, often overshadowing the heart and crotch aspects of the relationship.

An emotionally attractive relationship will pull on the heartstrings and draw you in because one yearns for affection, closeness, and intimacy that feels safe and nurturing and makes you feel understood. A person who can empathize with how you feel, regard your feelings, and be loving, kind, and gentle with your feelings can make you feel safe, willing to be vulnerable, and open to that type of love. In contrast, a person who is emotionally cold, distant, perhaps punishing, unable to express feelings or negative, critical, or withholding of their emotions can make you feel unsafe, vulnerable to hurt, fearful, untrusting, lonely, and perhaps isolated within the relationship. Again, as you realize that these are the person's heart connections, you can either move closer to them or flee emotionally to the loving arms of another in search of the missing empathy in your relationship.

How Self-Esteem Affects Outcomes

In my practice, I have often heard my clients say their partner "makes me feel like no one else ever has." This expression is used as a way of justifying their heart connection to their partner or as an excuse when seeking an affair outside of their relationship because they lack an emotional connection. Many a relationship has ended as a result of poor emotional connectivity; in other words, not being understood emotionally, being emotionally mistreated, or being treated abusively.

Whether one chooses to stay in an emotionally unfulfilling or emotionally abusive relationship has much to do with their self-esteem and how much they value their emotional world. When experiencing a loving, empathetic connection that fulfills you, you can either remain with the individual who provides this or run towards the individual who you believe will provide this. Granted, there are those individuals who will remain in an emotionally unfulfilling relationship, out of fear or low self-esteem, who do not think they are worthy of a genuinely caring, loving individual, or who do not trust that a person can love them unconditionally. But those individuals who feel worthy of love can and do often displace this need onto a different person when it no longer exists in their own inner world or when the emotional heart connection fails.

Sexual Connection

Sexual connection is so much more elusive to many a therapist in trying to explain the attraction, yet it is fairly common to hear that a relationship may fail because there is either no chemistry, the sex doesn't work or is unsatisfying, or in other instances, the sexual connection is not mutually gratifying. When a partner is concerned with satisfying their mate and is willing to attempt to give sexually, the relationship usually works better than one in which the individual is selfish and only concerned with gratifying their own needs.

Someone may seem sexually attractive through their words or deeds and emphasize their sexual prowess, but their ability to succeed sexually has more to do with their willingness to please rather than their bravado regarding performance. A crotch connection purely based on physical attraction will soon fail to satisfy if the connection is one-sided or un-giving. Again, there are those individuals who do not wish to or are not concerned with mutual gratification and may display either masochistic or sadistic traits in their sexuality. However, those are yet within the realm of individuals who will not be truly concerned with their crotch connection and will accept an individual not necessarily meeting their needs or provoking sexual incongruity as part of their sexual connection. An individual looking for a positive sexual connection will move towards one that is gratifying, either in fantasy or reality. They may look for it through an extramarital affair when it is missing or failing.

Head, Heart, Crotch Connections

Again, asking yourself the relevant questions of why, who, what, where, when, and which aspects of your connections you are relating to is necessary. For example, do you love or relate to all aspects of your partner's being, their head, heart, crotch, or are you just relating to parts of them? Identifying these areas of your connection can keep your relationship alive and obscure from failing. Over the course of the next several chapters, I will continue to address questions related to what I termed "The 6 W's of Connections."

CHAPTER 11

When Does a Relationship Begin to Fail?

There are several ways a relationship can start to fall apart. One way is failure through fantasy. The other is failure in reality or in one's actual world. Failure through fantasy occurs when one starts to think that we are missing or lacking a connection with our partner and think there must be someone out there who is better for us than our current one. Or we become aware of a deep dissatisfaction within one or more of our connections and start to believe we have to fulfill that missing connection.

Many of my patients in therapy have spoken of how they began to experience something wrong in their relationships without being able to identify what it was. As they took a deeper look at their concerns, they came to see that either they were perhaps not mentally compatible, not emotionally compatible, or finally, not sexually compatible. As soon as those thoughts occurred to them, if they did not attempt to address them with their partners, they began to fantasize that it could be remedied through a relationship with a different person.

How the Head Connection Fails

The ability to fantasize can help fulfill their wishes for a better connection, or it can be the start of a search for a connection outside of the relationship. At the level of fantasy, we can often assume and come to believe that there is a connection better and or more satisfying than the current one we have. For example, a relationship that lacks a mind connection begins to devalue the mindful, intellectual aspects of the person we are involved with and idealize the intellectual abilities of another. We find fault with how our partner may think, the content of their thoughts, or how they express their beliefs or thoughts.

Many a patient has expressed to me that they may have initially enjoyed their partner's mind and the way they expressed themselves, but with time, either they became disenchanted with their beliefs, or their beliefs changed, and it was no longer satisfying to hear what their partner's thoughts or beliefs were, often losing interest in either arguing or bantering with them. After many attempts to resolve or listen to differences with acceptance, they begin to devalue the difference and wish for sameness in thinking. Difference caused them anxiety and distress, and they long for someone who thinks more as they do. Differences cause conflict that can become unbearable, and the desire to flee becomes pressing.

This desire to escape conflict can lead to failure through fantasy. In fantasy, we become connected to someone who thinks and believes as we do. We wish to fulfill a sense of mental connectedness, and in that process, we start to devalue our mental connection to our partners and look to fulfill our connection with another. That is how a head connection begins to fail from fantasy.

How the Heart Connection Fails

A relationship that lacks a heart connection can begin to experience emotional disregard. A partner may become unsatisfactory when they no longer feel comforting, soothing, or satisfying. In fantasy, we begin to feel that our relationship lacks sensitivity and warmth or is indifferent to our feelings. We can begin to experience coldness, hostility, resentment, indifference, or other negative emotions. If we attempt to address the emotional disconnection, we can encounter barriers to change. We find out that our partners cannot emotionally relate in a more loving, caring manner or have no desire to express their emotions in a manner more consistent with our wishes. A relationship can fail when we have attempted to get our emotional needs met, but we begin to feel that our partners are unable or unwilling to be more empathetic, caring, loving, or expressive of their emotions in a way that is emotionally pleasing to us. Again, in fantasy, we begin to feel as if others can be more emotionally compatible, another who is not cold, indifferent, cruel, aggressive, or hostile to us.

How the Crotch Connection Fails

A relationship that lacks a crotch connection begins to fail when we think that there are others to whom we are more sexually attracted or begin to feel as if we are no longer attracted sexually to our partners. Thoughts that our partners are no longer sexually satisfying or are dissatisfied with sex can also lead to failure in fantasy. Feelings of sexual inadequacy or incompatibility can often be addressed but, when not resolved, can lead to failure through fantasy.

Feelings of sexual attraction can be characterized initially by lustful feelings, but lust can often wane and is usually replaced by loving, sexualized feelings. There are many opportunities to discuss sexual satisfaction, but people are often afraid to explore this as they think acknowledging it may mean an immediate dissolution of the relationship. Discussion of sexual feelings can lead to withdrawal or inhibition of sex or the possibility that sexual attraction has ended. This can be feared and is often avoided through fantasy.

Thinking that someone else can be more sexually satisfying can be easier than addressing the sexual inadequacy in the current relationship. One can escape the confrontation through sexual fantasy that is more fulfilling and seductive in nature. Sexual satisfaction is a difficult topic to explore because it can have so many determinants, but when sexual needs are not addressed, it can lead to distancing and eventual dissolution of the relationship. How and if we allow ourselves to address these feelings will determine if we will fight or flee the difficulty through fantasy or reality.

Failure in reality means we no longer fantasize about having our head, heart, and crotch connections met, but we go on to look for fulfillment outside of the relationship in the real world. Many patients have expressed the beginning phase of failure to encompass fantasy but then, subsequently, moved into reality. The fight or flight response in fantasy no longer works and proceeds to develop an external connection in the form of an affair. The affair is meant to flee the disconnection and fulfill magically, in some way, the missing connection we have with our current partners. The connection that is missing is searched for desperately in another. Whether it is a head, heart, or crotch dis-connect, the result can often be the failure to maintain the relationship.

How do you know if your relationship is strong or if you are experiencing a head, heart, crotch disconnect? I'll explore that further, providing answers and perhaps more questions in my next chapter.

CHAPTER 12

Denial: Heads in the Sand

"Denial was first described by the famed psychoanalyst Sigmund Freud, who described it as refusing to acknowledge upsetting facts about external events and internal ones, including memories, thoughts, and feelings."[20]

Denial is psychologically viewed as a coping mechanism that provides you with time to adjust to distressing situations or life's stressful challenges. According to Kendra Cherry, "denial is a type of defense mechanism that involves ignoring the reality of a situation to avoid anxiety. Defense mechanisms are strategies that people use to cope with distressing feelings. In the case of denial, it can involve not acknowledging reality or denying the consequences of that reality."[21]

What do we understand about denial as a defense mechanism in relationships? Do we need a certain amount of denial to sustain a connection, or is denial always unhealthy and ultimately ineffective for the relationship? More importantly, how does denial affect our head, heart, crotch connections?

---

20   Rui Miguel Costa, "Denial (Defense Mechanism)," SpringerLink (Springer International Publishing, January 1, 1970), https://link.springer.com/referenceworkentry/10.1007/978-3-319-28099-8_1373-1.
21   Kendra Cherry, "What Does It Mean When Someone Is in Denial?," Verywell Mind (Verywell Mind, May 29, 2021).

Head, Heart, Crotch Connections

There are two forms of denial that, in my experience, can influence our attachments. There is either healthy denial or unhealthy denial. The two types of denial serve to both keep us connected and disconnected at the same time. Unhealthy denial will keep us from acknowledging our disconnections, while healthy denial will serve to keep us connected to our partners despite the limitations/dissatisfaction we may experience.

A certain amount of healthy denial is needed to remain connected to our partners; otherwise, we would see all the flaws and the imperfection in our relationship, which would, in turn, create more disconnection. It seems like a paradox and contradictory in nature that they often serve the same function, but the healthy denial of a recognized problem can keep you as stuck as denial of the lack of a problem. To acknowledge a problem is often the beginning of dissatisfaction. But dissatisfaction can occur without acknowledgment of that very problem. Acknowledging that a connection may be missing can either set one in the direction of change, or they will accept the disconnection and learn to compensate for the loss.

Voicing or expounding upon as many aspects of our genuine thoughts and feelings breaks through unhealthy and healthy denial. So, if we are denying that either a connection is fulfilling us or that a connection is actually missing, we are prone to overlook or compensate for the missing connection.

Denial serves to keep anxiety contained, at bay. We can be anxious over things we recognize or unconsciously anxious over things we have failed to recognize/acknowledge. Nonetheless, anxiety is the first sign that something is wrong. When anxious, we clamorously question or experience unvoiced frustration. We know that anxiety is needed to make a change. The changes often needed when referring to the head, heart, crotch can only be addressed if first acknowledged and then addressed. Recognizing the flaws in our mind, body, and spirit connections is the beginning of the acceptance of them or the start of a retreat from them.

But how do you address them? I will attempt to explore this in my following discussion about describing your head, heart, crotch connections.

CHAPTER 13

Why Do Words Matter?

Do you have a head, heart, crotch connection? The answer to that is so individualized and can only be determined by exploring what you possess or fail to have in your current relationship. In my therapeutic work with clients, I recall that when an individual or couple would seek help with their relationship, I would sit down with them and start to explore their thoughts, emotions, and sexual desires. More often than not, many clients would experience difficulty explaining their thoughts, accurately sharing their emotions, or revealing their sexual concerns. Clients were often vague in how they would describe their problems, experiencing difficulty coming to terms with exactly what they were struggling with. I often needed to explore with them what examples of emotions were since they frequently lacked the ability to identify clearly or use sufficient words to describe their emotional states.

Clients would commonly say things like I'm sad, depressed, anxious, fearful or angry, frustrated, disillusioned, or disappointed in themselves or their partners, but failed to identify the range of emotions that either the partner had, which attracted them or turned them off. During the course of the therapy, I would ask them to identify what they most liked or respected about their partner's thoughts and then what they most liked about their partner's emotions. Exploring contrasting thoughts and emotional states was often the key to identifying what internal imagery was lacking, which could cause disconnection.

In exploring the thoughts that they respected or liked, it was determined that, more often than not, they had thought about them but hadn't taken the time to analyze them fully. Therefore, in therapy, I would ask them to describe their partner's ways of thinking. Would they use words like bright, verbal, intuitive, curious, intellectual, rational, flexible, sophisticated, or open-minded? Or would they utilize contrasting words like stubborn, bullheaded, irrational, dumb, unsophisticated, or ignorant, but needing help to describe further subtler states of thinking such as dull, naïve, sullen, gloomy, rigid, cynical, sarcastic, duplicitous, manipulative, or hostile.

My theoretical perspective behind soliciting specific, descriptive, differentiating words is that their use invokes internal imagery. Increased imagery amplifies experience and induces attachment. Attachment creates connections. The greater the experience of connection, the stronger the attachment. The stronger the attachment, the lesser the disconnect.

Helping clients refine and explore their different thought patterns and values was illuminating for them. They were able to clearly verbalize what they liked about their partner's thinking and what pained or disappointed them. Helping clients differentiate how their partner thinks and how it resonates with them or fails to resonate was often the key to helping them with their head connection by bringing them closer in understanding or having them identify why they drifted apart in thought and values.

Similarly, disconnection resulted when clients could not clearly and succinctly identify those feelings they were attracted to or felt most connected to. Exploring those range of feeling states helped them to see how being kind, humanistic, gentle, loving, patient, tender, cheerful, warm, forgiving, trusting, and comforting was in contrast to other negative emotional states like being aggressive, hostile, uncaring, hurtful, inpatient, withholding, cold, envious, vengeful, angry, distrustful, resentful, bitter or rancorous. Again, getting clients to identify the feelings they preferred versus the feeling states that caused distance and detachment was the key to working on a closer heart connection.

Exploring the Sexual Connection

Exploration of a sexual connection implies exploring perceived mutuality and if the partners feel that mutual satisfaction is important in the relationship. When we explored the crotch connection, words that came to mind for clients were often limited to either satisfying, pleasurable, loving, sexy, passionate or unsatisfying, boring, routine, unwilling, or unfulfilling. But more descriptive words for states of sexual relations were rarely, if ever, expressed, and mutuality was often overlooked. The therapy got them to see that there were other sexual needs or states that are equally descriptive and or necessary to consider, such as empathy, pleasure, willingness to please, giving-ness, safety, vulnerability, risks, and playfulness, in contrast to negative sexual experiences such as punishing, hurtful, self-involved, dispassionate, withholding, inattentive or unsatisfying.

Exploration of contrasting states was often the key to increasing fantasy and mental imagery, thus increasing the ability to clearly state and identify what went wrong or right about their sexual intimacy and connectedness.

Below are three different tables exemplifying contrasting affective and cognitive words as well as words for sexual expression.

Contrasting Descriptive Feeling States

Kind, humanistic, gentle	Punitive, aggressive, hostile
Loving, patient	Hateful, uncaring, impatient
Giving	Withholding
Affectionate	Cold, Unaffectionate
Carefree, cheerful, pleasant	Envious, unpleasant
Understanding, comforting, cordial	Jealous, grumpy
Forgiving	Vengeful, unforgiving
Happy	Depressed, angry, miserable
Trusting	Distrustful
Sympathetic, warmhearted, warm	Resentful, bitter, rancorous
Spiritual	Materialistic
Sensitive, passionate	Insensitive, unfeeling
Benevolent, permissive, protective	Petty, demanding, controlling

CHAPTER 13

Contrasting Descriptive Thinking States

Bright, informed	Dull, I
Verbal	Sullen, gloomy
Sophisticated	Unsophisticated
Intellectual	Dumb, ignorant
Curious, unconventional, uncommon	Apathetic, unexceptional, ordinary
Open-minded, optimistic	Closed-minded, cynical, sarcastic
Flexible	Stubborn, rigid, inflexible
Unbiased	Prejudiced, biased
Impartial	Judgmental
Rational, objective	Irrational, subjective
Truthful	Deceptive, duplicitous, manipulative
Thoughtful	Inconsiderate, thoughtless
Honest, noble	Dishonest, unethical, ignoble

Contrasting Descriptive Sexual Terms

Loving	Punishing
Empathic	Unsatisfying
Pleasing	Self-involved
Giving	With-holding
Safe, trusting	Vulnerable, hurtful, doubt
Pampered, indulged, cherished	Abused, intimidated
Seduced	Manipulated, coerced
Gratified, stimulated	Insulted, provoked
Pleasured	Pained

I once worked with a couple that claimed their intimacy was based on his willingness to please her sexually and that he was intellectually bright and emotionally sensitive as a person. She agreed for the most part with that description of him and that the intimate attachment was based on a "head, crotch, heart" order of connectedness for her. However, upon further exploration, it became clear that she felt differently. She thought that the order was "crotch, heart, head" and went on to explain how her partner was so willing to satisfy her sexually but to the exclusion of his own sexual gratification, often saying it wasn't important to him. My client said she thought that was originally quite novel and giving of him. But with the passage of time, my client began to see that he was selfishly withholding himself as opposed to being selfless and caring to her.

What had started as a sexual connection became a disconnection after she began to experience shame in the sexual union. She began to think that he was not really attracted to her and therefore didn't need to sexually satisfy himself, just satisfy her. Her shame was internalized, and she mentally moved from thinking it was a genuine crotch/body connection to a head, heart disconnect. What she thought was a head connection characterized by thoughtfulness and wish to please was replaced by the thought that it was actually self-centered, withholding intimacy, and was heart-wise punishing of her. She didn't feel loved by his expressed over-concern for her satisfaction, and the intimacy felt shameful to her as if she were using him for sex without a head or heart connection.

As the therapy explored their connections, she expressed a wish for a partner who gave of himself emotionally, who thoughtfully was not self-centered, and who was responsive sexually. She wanted and expressed a need for a better heart, head, crotch connection, in that order.

CHAPTER 14

When Familiarity Breeds Contempt

Although the expression "familiarity breeds contempt" is often attributed to Shakespeare, it was actually Geoffrey Chaucer, in his work, Tale of Melibee in the 1300s, who first coined the term. Nonetheless, when I think of it, I am reminded that Shakespeare may have also used the phrase, but more importantly, I think the word "familiarity" for him meant intimacy. Intimacy is the state of human interaction that can either bring you together or push you apart due to such familiarity. We can only love what we feel close to. We can not love something we do not know or do not feel close to. It is the reason why we cannot love a stranger. The closer we get to others, the more we can either love or hate them. Therefore, I believe that intimacy can breed contempt, but it can also breed genuine affection and deep love.

Intimacy involves getting to know someone really well, not just for who we want them to be, but for who they really are. The closer you get to someone, the more you can see their flaws and the more you can potentially dislike them. Equally understood is the more intimate you become, you can learn to overlook or see the humanity in their flaws and are willing to accept them. The latter outcome has a better chance of sustaining a connection to another than the former. If for you, intimacy breeds contempt, then it becomes difficult to sustain an attachment that will last.

Once we become truly intimate, we develop attachments that either flourish or fail to thrive. Much has been written within the field of psychology on attachment. Attachment theory describes attachments that can be described as either being secure or insecure, trusting or of a fearful nature, anxious-ambivalent, or avoidant in nature. A secure attachment allows for coming and going freely, without fear of abandonment, whereas a trusting attachment allows for vulnerability to be exposed without undue fear of harm. If you are interested in learning more about attachment theory and for a test to determine your attachment style, see Briana Macwilliams' online course entitled "Attachment in Adult Relationships."[22]

It has been noted that we don't see or experience people for what they really are but for what we want them to be, a projection of our own needs and desires. Therefore, exploring how we see or view ourselves and our partners results in a closer approximation of what we really wish for in our relationships. But can what we wish for be attained?

I once saw a female client who, when she initially started therapy, I asked what she saw in her partner. She described seeing brilliance in her partner's eye, but was not able to say what evidence was there for that perception nor what about their eye seemed brilliant. She went on to say that his eyes demonstrated tenderness and probably generosity. If his eyes showed tenderness, it meant he could be a good sexual partner. This was the basis for her head, heart, crotch connection to him. She thought she knew him, but her perceptions changed over time and with increased intimacy.

As time went on, she noticed that his generosity was limited to others and not with her. When asked what would happen when he wasn't being brilliant, generous, or tender, she acknowledged

---

[22] Briana MacWilliam, "Attachment in Adult Relationships Quiz," briannamacwilliam, 2021, https://quiz.brianamacwilliam.com/sf/a44c100a.

CHAPTER 14

resenting him for it. She would resent him, especially if he displayed it to others, not her. The more familiar she became with his ways, the more contempt she experienced. She did have to come to terms with the fact that she wanted him to be the things she had wished him to be, but the more she saw that he did not possess those characteristics, the more disillusioned she became. As the therapy progressed, she was able to voice to him her disappointment in his lack of generosity and tenderness, and he acknowledged that he had difficulty with intimacy and would work on overcoming this. She saw this as a possible good sign that he was still emotionally capable of empathy, and he was still cognitively smart.

This renewed perception helped her remain connected to him in mind, body, and spirit. Albeit, it exemplifies how one's wish for a certain type of connection can be displaced onto our partners whether or not they actually possess certain attributes, distorting the nature of our head, heart, crotch connection. What we wish for can only be attained when we realistically view our partners for who they are and not in some unconscious way wish that they be what we want them to be.

CHAPTER 15

Not All Connections Are Created Equal

Head, heart, crotch connections in relationships are characterized by fulfillments that are relative. Relationships that tend to work are those in which there is a relative satisfaction with those areas of connection needed to feel fulfilled. There is no perfect connection in which all areas are felt to be equally satisfying. Relationships are not static but often fluid in nature and are almost always changing. What was once extremely satisfying can remain so or can change over time.

In therapy, I would often ask clients to approximate their connection to their partners percentage-wise—the order of preference as well as the degree of importance. Clients would rarely say that their connection was equally distributed amongst the head, heart, and crotch. As you can imagine, connections were often described as "60-30-20" or "50-25-25" or "75-15-10" percent or any possible combination of percentages. But when we explored the area that possessed the least amount of connection, it was always the connection that pained them the most or was eventually identified as the most problematic and possible cause of their discord or failure in their relationship.

Asking a client to identify the order of preference often resulted in them identifying what level of connection needed work. So once they identified heart, head, crotch or heart, crotch, head or crotch, head, heart as their order of preference, we were able to determine what needed to be worked on or understood better to improve the relationship. The connection of least intensity was their area of vulnerability, the connection that could put their relationship most at risk. It was the identified area they needed to learn how to improve, should they risk loss, disconnection, or personal flight into fantasy. It felt like an easy task, a winning formula that clients could relate to and grasp as a tool in therapy that worked.

Is it necessary to have a complete head, heart, crotch connection for a relationship to work? The answer is no. There is no perfect connection or attachment to others. Attachments can be partially fulfilled and yet remain sufficiently rewarding to the individual. Needless to say, all connections are different, and what is most important to you may not be that important to another. But does overlooking or underestimating the value of a connection have implications for a relationship? Can you fail to recognize the significance of a particular connection? Can satisfaction in one connection compensate for the lack of another?

The Importance of Exploring Connections Fully

In my practice, I am reminded of the case of a young 30-year-old Asian-American female who came for therapy because of a failing relationship. She came from what she described as an intact immigrant family who had worked hard to establish themselves here in the USA. She described her parents as loving and kind but extremely permissive and tolerant of her demanding behaviors. She acknowledged the roots of her jealousy having been formed due to her parents treating her sister preferentially. She was born here and graduated from medical school.

CHAPTER 15

She was romantically involved with a young Anglo-American male who resided in her same town. He was working for the local police enforcement agency when they met. When she first came to therapy, she described a relationship that could be characterized as acrimonious. They fought a lot and had both emotional and physical altercations. She said she initially felt attracted to him because she had heard he was a police officer and other friends had dated him. When asked in therapy to explore her head, heart, crotch connection to him, she said she initially had felt a head connection to the idea of him being an officer and the value he would have placed on respecting the law. He appeared stern, authoritative, dominant, and law-abiding. This attracted her to him mentally.

She thought he could have been somewhat intelligent, despite not knowing his actual educational achievements. She then explained her sexual connection since she had heard that he was a good sexual partner from other women who had dated him. She thought he was especially physically attractive, describing him as tall, muscular, and with chiseled features. She found him to be very attractive physically. Lastly, she thought she could have had a heart connection because he was willing to date outside of his culture, meaning that he was open and not prejudiced but admittedly said that it was just based on supposition. The order of her connection was head, crotch, heart.

As the relationship progressed, she described her struggles sustaining her initial intimate attachment to him. She admits to becoming very jealous of him and his interactions with other women. She fell into drug and alcohol abuse as a way of managing her feelings of rage. She acknowledged initially being in a healthy denial about the actual character he possessed. As she got to know him more, the relationship became more volatile, with her accusing him of possible infidelity and him flaunting his interest in other females. She admitted to stalking-like behavior where she would show up at work or look through his cell phone for evidence of infidelity. As evidence surfaced, she could no longer control her emotions and would either threaten him with physical harm or threaten to hurt herself.

At this point in the therapy, I suggested she consider a psychiatric evaluation for possible medication, to which she agreed. She admitted to allowing herself to be so provoked by him that she no longer could control her behaviors. She was becoming clearly depressed and agitated to the point of mental confusion. With time and therapy, she regained her composure after exploring what each connection meant to her and how the initial attachments she made faltered over the course of the relationship. She described how she no longer respected him for being an officer since she noticed that he was not fair, nor did he treat all civilians equally. He was sometimes cruel and foul-mouthed with some while being obsequious and lenient with others. He valued conservative views of policies, which she viewed progressively and more leniently in line with her view of herself as a helping professional. Her head connection began to wane as she saw other sides of him that were displeasing to her.

Her sexual connection remained fairly intact since she said he continued to want to have sexual relations. But she no longer trusted that he was monogamous as he claimed to have been.

She initially had described her partner as a gentle, respectful man who spoke softly and was honest and agreeable. With time in therapy, she began describing his character with words like manipulative, calculating, cunning, aggressive, hostile, and often devious. Her heart connection was affected by his innumerable cruel statements about her lack of intelligence, despite her graduating from medical school. He would demean her and speak negatively of her cultural background. She felt offended by his biased views but never came to acknowledge the prejudice and racism behind them fully. She had believed that since he was willing to date outside of his race that this meant he could not be racist or prejudiced. She admitted she was in denial about this, and her rationalizations kept her from seeing it or disrupting the connection.

Concerning her heart connection, she noticed that he was initially engaging, tender, and loving in bringing her gifts and bringing her home to meet his mom. She felt safe and loved by his mom but did not always feel safe with him. He would express his frustration with her in raging bouts of anger. He would curse and demean her in public. She longed for the initial gentler expressions of caring but saw that his emotions harbored intense feelings of animosity, disdain, and condescension.

Within time and after exploring fully her connections to her partner, she saw that her attachment was flawed and her relationship had failed. She no longer maintained a solid head, heart, crotch connection. She said that it had switched towards the end of the relationship, transforming itself into solely a crotch connection at best and no longer experiencing any genuine head or heart connection.

Months after leaving this relationship, she met another person who she considered could be a better connection.

I will discuss this case further when I explore how to succeed and overcome disconnection. I will reveal how she came to establish a new relationship, successfully analyzing her attachment, and was able to sustain a different head, heart crotch connection.

In my clinical experience, those persons who have identified their relative satisfaction with their connections have managed to remain in their relationships and fight rather than flee. Those who had not thought about the quality of their relatedness have failed to sustain the relationship and often have prematurely escaped it either in fantasy or in reality. Those who identify the flaws in their connections can often end an unhealthy attachment.

CHAPTER 16

What Is the Nature of Your Head, Heart, Crotch Connection?

At this point in your reading, you may have accepted the notion that connections made at the level of the head, heart, and crotch influence our attachments. If so, you will want to know how to recognize your HHC connection and what is the nature of your connections. To do so, you will need to begin by identifying what your core values are. What do you believe in, what are your ideas, and what do you tend to espouse mentally? Does what you believe in and hold dear conflict with your partner's beliefs or perspectives? Do they often clash, or are they more often compatible? If they clash, how much do you mentally struggle with accepting your partner's perspective? Does it cause you discomfort or pain or just annoyance? Or do you experience pleasure in listening to your partner's perspective, which creates a sense of pride and admiration? Are you able to agree to disagree and still remain mentally attached, or have you begun to disconnect?

Head, Heart, Crotch Connections

After identifying your core values, are you still able to respect your partner's values, or do you wish to avoid or flee from them? The ability to respect and admire your partner will determine your ability to sustain a positive head connection. A positive mental connection can allow you to endure the differences in beliefs we may often possess, yet not cause us displeasure or a desire to flee. When your differences become painfully difficult to bear, that is how a disconnection begins, and we flee to fantasy or in reality in search of a more perfect head connection.

Our heart connection is determined by you knowing your genuine feelings and reactions to experiences, and once expressed, how much your partner is able to accept your emotional states without judgment, criticism, or belittling of you. Does your partner express emotions that are pleasing to you in response to your feelings? Do the emotions they experience translate into a sense of loving, empathy, and trust in you? Or does their emotional perspective cause you pain, anguish, and suffering? Heart connections that feel abusive, manipulative, controlling, critical, shaming, judgmental, or punitive often cause displeasure and can become a source of estrangement. We slowly, over time, become more distant if unable to resolve or improve our partner's emotional reactions to us.

A heart connection that is understanding, kind, gentle, empathetic, respectful, and loving generates trust and safety. The feeling of trust and safety with our partner is what allows us to remain emotionally attached.

As you identify these feelings in yourself and your partner, what you need to ask yourself is whether you are able to remain feeling safe, trusting, loving, and connected. Does the relationship feel safe to discuss your thoughts, feelings and sexual wishes? Does it allow for vulnerability to be experienced safely and without fear? Or do you feel unsafe, untrusting, and unloved, perhaps growing increasingly disconnected?

The nature of your heart connection will be determined by your ability to accept your partner's emotional expressions. Your wish to remain attached rather than flee will be influenced by how satisfied you feel in your heart connection.

CHAPTER 16

Now I am sure you may want to know how to explore your sexual connection. Your sexual connection to the degree that you feel more or less intimate with your partner is determined by your partner's willingness to mutually please you and themself in the relationship. It can often start by just asking yourself if it feels pleasing, but going beyond mere pleasure, you could determine how mutually gratifying it is. Are you both concerned with it feeling pleasurable and joyful? Or does the sexual experience leave you feeling empty or sexually used in some way? Do you freely give of yourself, or do you feel manipulated into sex? Does it produce a feeling of fulfillment and joy, or did you feel shame, disgust, or unhappiness? Do you wish to re-experience sex with your partner, or do you wish to flee in fantasy or perhaps in reality?

Answering these questions honestly can lead to a heightened sense of attachment or the realization that you perhaps struggle with your sexual connection. Exploring and voicing dissatisfaction with your partner can lead to discussing areas of needed improvement. Your partner's willingness to listen to your concerns should be a barometer for success or failure.

If you feel demeaned, disrespected, or abused by the sexual nature of your connection, this will characterize the true nature of your sexual attachment. The feeling that something about your sexual connection feels irreparable should be a red flag that perhaps you lack a genuine attachment. But if your sexual attachment and your partner's willingness to explore it leads to openness and increased mutuality then you can be assured that the connection is a positive one.

Sexual pleasure that is mutual and gratifying is the goal. Sexual connections that are degrading, humiliating, or unsatisfying often lead to a flight rather than fight reaction. The degree to which you are willing to describe your sexual experience honestly will determine how you perceive the level of intimacy and success or failure of your crotch connection. The sexual act itself is not as important in determining the success of your connection as is the mutually gratifying aspects of it. A positive crotch connection is established when both partners feel sexually satisfied.

Importance of Identifying the Nature of Your Attachment

I want to reintroduce the case of my patient, who left her first partner and succeeded in overcoming a relationship disconnection. Months after leaving the first relationship, my client met a man from her parents' native Southeast Asia. She was initially hesitant since she had negative views toward people from her own cultural background. Nevertheless, she allowed herself to get to know him and described what she was attracted to in him.

She voiced thinking she may have encountered a heart, head, crotch connection since her first impression was that he was gentle, respectful, soft-spoken, and notably bilingual. That was her described head connection. She saw him in his military uniform and again thought he was gentleman-like, perhaps protective, and had an engaging persona and pleasant smile. She felt emotionally attracted to him. Finally, she said he was handsome and appeared physically fit, so she experienced a sexual attraction but had no real knowledge of him intimately.

As this relationship progressed, she was more able to expound on her perceptions. She had come to view him as quite intellectually bright and perceptive. He had graduated from the military academy and had plans to rise within the ranks. He was emotionally quite sensitive and expressed his love easily without fear or reservation. He was emotionally careful in his verbalizations, making sure not to offend. She felt trust in him and safe around him. She thought that he had attained this level of empathy as a result of being an only child raised by a single mother. She witnessed the love he had for his mother and the care with which he treated her. She said he was a passionate lover and was always concerned with their mutual satisfaction in sexual relations. She voiced having attained a genuine heart, head, crotch connection to her satisfaction.

When problems began in their relationship, it was again because of her jealousy and having looked through his cell phone for any possible evidence of infidelity. She found that while deployed, he was viewing pornographic sites. She confronted him, and he said

CHAPTER 16

it was better to view pornography rather than look outside of the relationship for sexual gratification. She found this disturbing and continued to question him about it. It reached the point where he could no longer tolerate her displays of jealousy and threatened to leave the relationship. She described having lost her heart connection to him, even though she felt a strong head and crotch connection; she still admired him intellectually and felt sexual passion. In therapy, she admittedly accepted the notion that she had damaged the heart connection and would need to regain his trust through empathetic expressions of deep emotional concern and compassion for him. She was unwilling to lose the person she believed she had attained a head, heart, crotch connection with.

When asked what she thought was his head, heart, crotch connection to her, she could reflect and say that he had a head connection to her intelligence, respecting what she had accomplished academically. He believed that she was loving and kind despite her jealousy, and despite her being overweight, he found her sexy and attractive, and it did not interfere with their intimate sexual relations. She realized that his heart connection may have changed towards her when he witnessed how she "flipped out" emotionally and when he perceived "the demon in her" that had surfaced. She knew that there was a heart disruption when he observed that behavior.

However, she believed that since he was so forgiving and kindhearted, he could rebound and start anew. She thought it was good that she saw how angry he could get because it gave her a more balanced view of him, but it did not create a disruption or disconnection in her attachment to him. They overcame the emotional disconnection and attempted to regain what they felt they had lost. They continued in therapy and succeeded in maintaining their union.

I believe that her case exemplifies how working on the concept of mind, body, and spirit attachment can help to, first, identify the exact nature of your attachment and, second, how to redress a failing or changing attachment. As she uncovered and verbalized the true feelings of lack and want in her first relationship, she was able to transform her view of the relationship and distance herself

Head, Heart, Crotch Connections

emotionally from her initial attachment impression. She developed a clearer understanding of what was missing in her head and heart connection, allowing her to disengage slowly. Seeing why she no longer sustained a head and heart connection was painful for her but necessary to identify what went wrong—seeing what went wrong allowed her to fantasize about what she wanted in her next relationship. She came to see how a fuller mind, body, and spirit connection would be needed to experience a secure attachment and feel love.

CHAPTER 17

When Trauma Affects Our HHC Connection

Most head, heart, crotch connections that work are created by relatively healthy attachments. But what happens to the ability to connect when the attachment is affected by early mental, emotional, or physical abuse? Dr. Sigmund Freud's daughter, Dr. Ana Freud, was a famous psychoanalyst who worked with abandoned and traumatized children in orphanages during World War II. She provided the therapeutic community with a deeper understanding of how trauma created by abandonment, abuse, or neglect affects our ability to connect. Her experiences led her to define the defense mechanism she called "Identification with the Aggressor."[23] When a person has been traumatized as a result of abuse, they learn to accept and perceive the abuse as normal. Love looks like abuse. Love becomes tainted with aggression, either emotional or physical.

They learn to identify with aggression and internalize what they were exposed to. Love was shown as angry, violent, and hurtful

---

23 Anna Freud, *The Ego and Mechanisms of Defence* (London: Hogarth Press and Institute of Psycho-Analysis, 1937).

emotions. If your form of love was imbued with aggression and anger, you inevitably would be confused by genuine, caring, empathetic forms of love. It would be foreign to you. If you are not used to loving relations, you will not be familiar with them, and they will confuse you. You may experience distrust and be leery of them. This would create difficulty in normal connection and possibly result in disconnection. I mention this because patients suffering from trauma often come to therapy with extensive histories of childhood abuse, neglect, or abandonment. Coming to terms with childhood trauma and the interference it creates for adult relations is often painstakingly difficult.

Initial connections can be made but often are affected as the relationship proceeds. For example, unresolved feelings from childhood can be displaced onto our current connections leading one to falsely believe that our connections are not good ones and that we must end them out of fear or distrust. When this is the situation, therapy serves to help identify for the client how trauma is affecting their HHC connection. The ability of the therapist to help the client see the negative effects of trauma will help determine if the client can attain a healthier HHC connection.

Determine If Your HHC Connection Is Positive or Negative

I recall a client who came for therapy and voiced having come from an emotionally abusive parental background but claimed she had a good head, crotch, heart crotch connection with her partner. She voiced appreciating his mind because the husband was a brilliant professor and sexually because he could be passionate and affectionate, but emotionally he was an angry, hostile person. He was described as a rageaholic. He saw anger in many situations where anger may not have been present.

My patient felt she understood his anger because she was raised with rage and aggression. After many years of dealing with it, she felt she could no longer tolerate it. She claimed she could no longer sustain a positive heart connection and went in search of a man who was not so angry. She said she wanted calm and peace but admittedly was not used to it. It was a fantasy she had of attaining a gentler partner.

With time, her own unfamiliarity and distrust of kindness, which she was not used to, led her to leave the fantasied partner as well. She always distrusted his kindness, and any sign of annoyance or anger on his part only proved to her that he was really hiding his true nature and was possibly abusive. The projection of her childhood trauma onto her relationships was rooted in both unhealthy denial, which kept her tethered to her first husband, and also identifying with aggression, in which she abandoned her second partner, fearing perceived aggression where none existed.

In my experience, most cases in which one explores the connections made to the HHC do not lead to the dissolution of the relationship as in the above case. On the contrary, most times, exploring the HHC connection has had beneficial effects and has managed to overcome risk factors or areas of vulnerability for the relationships.

The Benefits of Exploring the HHC Connection

The exploration of head, heart, crotch connections with clients is not only affected by denial or trauma but is also influenced by advancing in chronological age. In our youth, we can often be impetuous and intolerant in our relatedness, and this can result in quick endings of relationships without a full analysis—quick to say what we love or what we can't stand about the person. Youthful individuals can often enter a love relationship idealizing the other person, and you'll hear things like, "Oh, he's perfect, so sweet and loving and smart," for example.

What happens when we first meet someone, and need to idealize them to make a connection, is that we fail to see reality and the person's true nature. The fear of devaluing them immediately makes one initially idealize the other. If we begin by devaluing, we fail to idealize and connect. But connecting too quickly by idealizing the other doesn't give us enough time to truly get to know the person.

Head, Heart, Crotch Connections

In therapy with my clients, I have gotten them to explain what they mean by "I really like them." Often, when that is mentioned, it is because they have usually failed to really examine what they like or admire about the person. Quick yet vague responses without much elaboration often occur in youthful couplings until I start to dig in a bit and ask questions related to the head, heart, and crotch. Even then, I may get a vague response like, "He is really smart," or "He is so sensitive," or "He has a great body and would probably be great in bed." My job becomes working on each part of the mind, body, and spirit connection to see how deep a connection has actually been made versus just the superficial expressions of love/desire elaborated.

In my practice, I recall a 35-year-old married female client who said, "It was his eyes" when I asked her what she first noticed about her partner. She was initially unable to elaborate what about his eyes but, upon deeper questioning, said they looked kind and gentle. This was clearly based on a wish for him to be kind and gentle since she didn't really know him, nor could she confirm that he was actually like that. She first connected at the heart level by looking at his eyes and assuming kindness, then at the head by saying he was an intellectual college student, so he must be smart. Finally, she mentioned that he was on the soccer team, so he must be physical and have many female admirers.

My client clearly had created in her mind a fantasized head, heart, crotch connection long before testing out any real mind, body, spirit awareness. Her need to project onto him a kind, gentle, intellectual, sports-like prowess was her first expressed wish, which was generated by her unconscious desire for him to be those things. As time went on, she began to see that although he was intelligent and displayed physical sexuality through sport, he was not as kind and gentle as she had originally thought. He could be rough, insensitive, and, at times, cruel in his handling of others.

When asked what was her head, heart crotch connection like months after dating, it became clearer to her that she remained sexually connected to his prowess but was experiencing difficulty with her head and heart connection to him. She thought he was bright and intellectual enough and could admire him for it but was often disappointed in how he could be cruel to others and treat others with disregard or outright disrespect. Her head connection remained strong, but she was losing her heart connection due to so many incidents of emotional discord and pain. The heart attachment had started to disconnect. Her attempts to get him to see his cruelty was often met with mockery and invalidation. (See *Words That Hurt Words That Heal* by Joseph Telushkin.)[24]

After years of trying to get her original unconscious wish for someone with gentle, kind eyes, she began to give up on attaining that projected wish. She would confront and plea for him to consider the effect his mean words had on others and their relationship but to no avail. He seemed to enjoy his ability to be cruel and the power he would feel by demeaning others. After years of therapy, when she realized he would not or could not change, she came to the realization that she could only change herself, not him. Shortly after that awareness occurred to her, she began to fantasize about being with someone who had kind words to say. This change started in fantasy, and unbeknownst to her or me, she started looking outside her relationship for a gentle, kinder male figure.

She started attending poetry readings and met a young poet she described as sensitive, verbal, insightful, and kind. This started off as a friendship, but with ongoing encounters, it soon developed into a deep heart connection that caused her to experience the loss of her emotional connection to her then-existent husband. Therapy proceeded to the point where she began to verbalize how she could no longer be with a cruel man and how she had yearned to flee and escape from him to the arms of someone else more loving and gentle. She continued to struggle internally for months with the idea that she would have to leave her husband because she had lost her head and heart connection to him even though, sexually, she still felt connected to him.

---

[24] Joseph Telushkin, *Words That Hurt, Words That Heal* (New York, NY: W. Morrow and Co., 1995), https://www.amazon.com/Words-That-Hurt-Heal-Revised/dp/0062896377.

Head, Heart, Crotch Connections

She began to realize that her sexual intimacy was based on their mutual attraction and level of passion but also on a prior myth of sexual prowess, which her friends had ingrained into her about sports figures.

After all was said and done, she said she had a crotch connection but lacked the head and heart. She believed it was an area of her life so missing that she could no longer live without it. She yearned more for a closeness deemed mind and spirit rather than body-focused. Within two months, she asked her partner for a divorce and pursued a relationship with the male poet. She acknowledged that the body connection was not as strong as with her husband, but she felt it was strong and pleasing enough to withstand the test of time. She voiced her heart connection to be most gratifying and the head connection to feel complimentary to her way of thinking about others. Finally, she gleefully admitted to having attained a head, heart, crotch connection that she placed at 35 percent head, 40 percent heart, and 25 percent crotch.

As I had said earlier, not all connections are created equal, but this was the right proportion of connections that worked for her and the needed level of intimacy which sustained her attachment to him. The heart connection had won out. This was her perceived perfect union. What's important to recognize is that what is considered perfect for one person is clearly not perfect or near perfect for another. I will re-emphasize the notion that all connections are relative and not created equally.

CHAPTER 18

What's Needed to Make a Good Head, Heart, Crotch Connection?

Can you overcome disconnection and succeed?

What if your connections need improvement?

How do you work on achieving a good head, heart, crotch connection?

If your connections are faltering, it's time to work on them. You may be asking what would be required of you to evaluate your head, heart, crotch connection, or equally of value, your partner's connection to you. First and foremost, have you taken the time to ask yourself what type of individual you are most attracted to? Is it the intellectual type, the emotional type, or the sexual type? What do you look for in others? This answer will help you define what you most value in your head, heart, crotch connections. Is one area weak, and does it overshadow another? Do you have an order of preference? Is the order interchangeable, or is it fixed? Can one stronger connection compensate for a weaker connection? The clearer you are on these questions, the more able you are to assess your head, heart, crotch connection.

Have you examined the image you project? Is it your intellect, your emotionality, or your sexuality? If so, what image does your partner relate to in you?

How do you know if you are an HHC connection for your partner? You could assume you are well connected with your partner, but if you are concerned or doubting your connection, the best way is to inquire. What makes you an HHC connection for your partner? Again, you have to inquire. You need to find out how they relate to your thoughts, feelings, and sexual relationship.

The formula is fairly easy to understand:

- A head connection exists when we are intrigued and or can admire our partner's way of thinking.
- A heart connection exists when we feel safe among the feelings expressed by our partner's feelings towards us.
- A sexual connection exists when we feel mutually satisfied by the sexual encounter with our partners.

The formula also applies to your partner's attraction to you as well. Where do their attractions for you lie? Do they love the connection they have made to your head, your heart, or your crotch? What would be their order of preference towards you?

Upon exploring these questions, any area you determine has the least connection would indicate the area of greatest vulnerability for your relationship. It would be considered the weakest link in your connection, so to speak.

Overcoming Disconnection and Addressing the Area of Vulnerability in Your Relationship

The order of your attachment can reveal the area of most vulnerability in your relationship and the connection which requires the most attention. If your heart connection is the weakest, it requires that you determine the exact nature of the disconnect and work on

CHAPTER 18

improving the connection. It may require that you identify the emotion or feeling that is lacking and attempt either through fantasy to recreate the emotion or through honest discussion to speak about the vulnerability or lack and get your partner to acknowledge the feeling state that is missing or divergent from yours. Using as many descriptive words to identify feelings will help to overcome the difficulty with an emotional heart connection. If you struggle with a head connection, explore values and beliefs you either share in common or those in which you differ. If you struggle with a sexual connection, explore the feelings of perceived mutual satisfaction that may be missing or overlooked.

Once the weaker connection is identified, it should be fully explored with the goal of increasing the connection. Employing specific substantive words to describe the connection state should help create a fuller experience. The fuller the emotional experience, the greater the attachment becomes. As the attachment increases, it amplifies the intimate nature of your connection. You should no longer experience a heightened sense of disconnection.

But what does it actually require of you? It entails exploring the words you ascribe to your connections. How do you talk about your partner and your head, heart, crotch connection to them? What do you say about your head, heart, crotch connection? Are the words you use creating or hindering and impeding a connection? Our mental representations are affected by how one chooses to view the other person at any particular point in time. So when we first meet someone, we tend to idealize the other as a way of attaching. When we no longer wish to remain attached, we tend to devalue the other. These are the defenses we tend to employ in the process of becoming connected or disconnected to or from the other.

In psychology, the mechanism of splitting is a common defense mechanism. It is defined as categorizing people or beliefs as either all good or bad, all positive or negative. It is the tendency to think in black and white terms without seeing the shades of gray in situations, thereby failing to integrate the complexities and nuances of life into one cohesive whole. If you see the actions and motivations of your partner as all good or bad, this can lead to excessive frustration and anger, often resulting in the person losing admiration for the partner and thinking that they are not worthy of them. When splitting is applied to our interpersonal relationships, it is characterized by defenses like devaluation and idealization. When our inner representations of others are split, it can look as if things are either all good or bad, split along the lines of black and white thinking, influencing how connected or disconnected we become.

What Mental Representations Are You Holding Onto?

The idealization of the other keeps one connected—the devaluing of the other results in disconnection. You may already be with the person who is perfect for you, but you do not perceive it because you are allowing splitting to take hold. When searching for the perfect union and preventing disconnection, you must avoid utilizing splitting as a defense in your relationship and in your internal object representations. The other person must not be made to be all good or all bad. A balanced view of the person's mental, emotional, or sexual attributes allows you to remain connected.

What does it take to overcome a less than perfect or imperfect connection to find a more perfect union? It requires that an individual explore the words they ascribe to their mental, emotional, and sexual connections. So, for example, if you are ascribing all negative words to describe your (mental/cognitive) head connection or your emotional or sexual connection, you may need to reframe your perception cognitively. If you see your partner as cognitively dull, ignorant, or bullheaded, recall experiences when they were open-minded, intuitive, or insightful. This results in going from an insecure attachment to a more secure attachment—the more positive the imagery, the greater the potential to outbalance the negative images in your mind.

The more you can allow yourself to see the positive attributes rather than the contrasting negative ones, the more the attachment progresses towards a secure rather than insecure attachment. In therapy, this is referred to as cognitive reframing, where you reframe your thoughts or beliefs to explore what counter-belief may serve you better, i.e., to hold onto resentment or to forgive. When you view your partner as suspicious, and untrusting, you could reframe this view to incorporate the possibility that they may be cautious and fearful or avoidant under certain circumstances. The perceptions you believe can allow you to increase your connection as opposed to limiting it.

This is not to say that one denies negative attributes. But to increase your connection, you may need to rethink some of your perceptions converting them into positive ones, thereby allowing for a secure attachment rather than an insecure attachment based only on negative perceptions. A balanced view of your thoughts is required to remain connected in a healthy way. Therefore, a person may need to see that their partner is not always bull-headed, suspicious, or distrusting, but that they can also be the opposite: trusting, caring, thoughtful, and insightful. This change in cognitive perception often results in remaining connected. Conversely, if you cannot reframe your perceptions, you will remain disconnected and feel insecure in your attachment.

The same concept applies to your perceptions of your partner's emotions and your sexual perceptions as well. To overcome an emotional disconnection, an individual would need to observe what words they are ascribing to their heart connection. If you view your partner as emotionally unfeeling, withholding, punitive, or unaffectionate, are you stuck in that perception, or can you recall times when you viewed them as more passionate, giving, kind, and affectionate? Are you able to cognitively reframe those perceptions enough to see that maybe there were aspects that you may be underestimating or misperceiving?

Can you view them in those contrasting emotional states? If you can alter your perception, should it be based on extreme views, perhaps influenced by all black or white-type thinking, then maybe a change in feeling state can occur, with a resulting move towards re-connection. If you cannot change your perception because what you perceive continues to be negative, then it would naturally result in an emotional disconnection and further distancing. Essentially it is a matter of determining if the negative perceptions out-shadow or out-weigh the positive ones and if you cannot reconcile the dissonance or discomfort it creates in you.

To overcome a sexual disconnection, one would again have to examine what words you use to describe your sexual experience. Is it currently described as being unsatisfying, selfish, withholding, unpleasurable, or coercive, or are you able to describe it as loving, giving, stimulating, pleasurable and trusting? To what degree can you create or recall more satisfying sexual experiences? To what degree have you given up on seeking sexual experiences from your partner which are pleasurable? What value do you place on sexual gratification? Is it more or less important than intellectual and emotional connection? Can the experience of mutual gratification be achieved or relived? All relevant questions to consider when exploring your sexual connection. In the pursuit of a more perfect union the ultimate determining indicator being if the sexual connection is mutually gratifying or not.

Substantive Words for a Better Attachment

The use of substantive words identifying contrasting states to describe the nature of your head, heart, crotch connection is extremely valuable in improving your relationship. In contrast, the use of idealization and devaluation in the process of splitting your internal perceptions is not conducive to a healthy head, heart, or sexual connection. Splitting internal representations, where your perceptions are either all good or bad and where you identify only negative attributes and fail to see positive ones, can lead to disconnection. The opposite is also true; seeing only the positive and none of the negative attributes can keep you in denial and connected in an unhealthy manner. Defensive splitting should be avoided to remain connected and if you wish to sustain a healthy attachment.

If you are struggling with approximating toward a better attachment because you view the attributes negatively, you will continue to experience difficulty in one or more of your connections which has ramifications for your relationship. Again, this doesn't mean you have to deny the difficulties, but a balanced view of the good

CHAPTER 18

and bad qualities with the balance in the direction of more positive ascriptions will allow for a better connection. We as humans are all flawed, but the healthiest state is one of balance where we perceive the negative and the positive, the good and the bad, where one contrasting state doesn't overshadow or outweigh the other. We need to achieve balance in our mental, emotional, and sexual experiences.

When your described attachments allow you to feel a balanced, positive, mind, body, spirit connection, you know that you have succeeded in attaining a healthy head, heart, crotch connection.

Rating Scale to Determine Level of Connection

To help you get a sense of your personal level of connection and your partner's connection to you, I have devised the following rating scale, which you can utilize. It is not a formal, research-based questionnaire, but think of it as a tool you can employ to help determine the nature of your connection and where you may need to address changes for improvement in your relationship. Experience is subjective, fluid, and ever-changing, so the scale is purely descriptive, experiential in nature, only meant to determine what attachment you are currently feeling and not to assess any future sense of connection.

Connections do and will change over time. They are subject to change and often change during the current course of a relationship and certainly in any future relationship. Couples will never experience the exact same connection towards one another, nor can two separate relationships ever experience the same connection. There is no replication of connections since every relationship will present its own unique attachments. No two relationships will ever be rated in exactly the same way. This is what makes each relationship so unique and intimacy so special in its attainment.

Guide to Interpreting Rating Scale

Each "very disconnected" response on the scale would indicate the heightened area of vulnerability for your relationship. It would be considered the weakest link in your connections. "Very connected" responses would indicate the strength within your connections and the lesser need for any amelioration in your relationship.

The greater the connection, the more the attachment. The greater the disconnection, the lesser the attachment.

HEAD, HEART, CROTCH CONNECTION RATING SCALE

For each item on the scale below, rate your connection.

Rate your Head Connection to your partner:

Very Connected	Somewhat Connected	Neither Connected nor Disconnected	Somewhat Disconnected	Very Disconnected

Rate your Heart Connection to your partner:

Very Connected	Somewhat Connected	Neither Connected nor Disconnected	Somewhat Disconnected	Very Disconnected

Rate your Crotch (Sexual) Connection to your partner:

Very Connected	Somewhat Connected	Neither Connected nor Disconnected	Somewhat Disconnected	Very Disconnected

Rate your partner's Head Connection to you:

Very Connected	Somewhat Connected	Neither Connected nor Disconnected	Somewhat Disconnected	Very Disconnected

Rate your partner's Heart Connection to you:

Very Connected	Somewhat Connected	Neither Connected nor Disconnected	Somewhat Disconnected	Very Disconnected

Rate your partner's Crotch (Sexual) Connection to you:

Very Connected	Somewhat Connected	Neither Connected nor Disconnected	Somewhat Disconnected	Very Disconnected

CHAPTER 18

Once you have rated your connections on the above scale, you can determine where your strengths and weaknesses lie in your relationship. This will help you focus on the areas needing improvement moving forward.

CHAPTER 19

Why Does Age Affect Our Perception of a Head, Heart, Crotch Connection?

Have you heard the expression, "Listen to your elders not because they're always right, but they have more experience at being wrong"? Going through life and experimenting with different attachments often leads to changes in the nature of our connections. Our values and connections are not unalterable. Whereas values are usually fairly consistent throughout our lifetime, they don't have strict boundaries. As we move through life, our values can change. For example, a value placed on work and success, as measured by money and status, may have driven you when you were younger, but after you marry and have a family, balance in your work life may become your emotional priority. As your definition of success changes, so can your values change.

With age comes a certain level of wisdom. As we age, we grow emotionally, intellectually, and physically. We look back at our values and re-evaluate what we achieved or believed in our youth.

Changes often occur as we develop and what we once loved or admired as a younger person often changes as we mature. That is not to say that some individuals do not struggle more than others in changing and maturing; nevertheless, individuals do change. What we cherished as a younger person, we may no longer esteem as we age. Our tastes change as we mature, as does our knowledge base and sometimes our values as well.

If in your youth you valued sexual expansiveness as a measure of your sensuality, in older age, you may change and measure it by fidelity and years of commitment as opposed to increasing diversity. Again, this is not to say that it is the case for everyone, but most. What we wanted and wished for at the age of twenty usually differs by age fifty. As a result, our wish for certain types of connections may change, and the preference order of those connections may also change.

As we age, we can increase the ability to tolerate inequality in our connection areas more than when we are young. In our youth, we can be more fixed in our head, heart, crotch connections, believing that what is most valued is fixed and not transmutable. With age often comes experience and the realization that our connections change and that our relationships cannot be totally in every way rewarding or fulfilling. We ultimately accept limitations in ourselves and our partners.

Acceptance of inequality in our connections is part of maturity. With increasing age, tolerance to frustration, impulse control, and the ability to delay immediate gratification is usually more highly developed. Regretfully when it is not, we are often doomed to repeat the errors of our youth and move on precipitously to the dissolution of our relationships in search of the elusive, more perfect union.

Nonetheless, it is with the hope and expectation that regardless of age, a person can create attachments that sustain greater intimacy through improved connections. The job of improving connections *is* achievable. The search for the perfect union may seem daunting; however, it is embraceable for those who wish for it. What may seem an elusive endeavor can be achieved with the knowledge attained from exploring head, heart, crotch connections. This knowledge has the power to result in overcoming difficulties and finding success in search of your perfect union.

Appendix A: List of Common Values

Accuracy	Diligence	Generosity	Obedience
Achievement	Discipline	Goodness	Openness
Altruism	Discretion	Grace	Order
Ambition	Diversity	Growth	Patriotism
Assertiveness	Economy	Happiness	Perfection
Balance	Effectiveness	Hard Work	Positivity
Belonging	Efficiency	Health	Practicality
Boldness	Elegance	Helping	Professional
Calmness	Empathy	Honesty	Prudence
Carefulness	Enjoyment	Honor	Quality
Commitment	Enthusiasm	Humility	Reliability
Community	Equality	Independence	Resourceful
Compassion	Excellence	Ingenuity	Restraint
Competition	Excitement	Inquisitiveness	Rigor
Consistency	Expertise	Insightfulness	Security
Contentment	Exploration	Intelligence	Selflessness
Contribution	Expressiveness	Intuition	Self-reliance
Concern	Fairness	Joy	Sensitivity
Control	Faith	Justice	Simplicity
Cooperation	Family-oriented	Leadership	Spontaneity
Courtesy	Fidelity	Legacy	Stability
Decisiveness	Fitness	Love	Strength
Democracy	Fluency	Loyalty	Success
Dependability	Focus	Mastery	Thoughtfulness
Determination	Freedom	Merit	Understanding
Devoutness	Fun	Mercy	Vision

Appendix B: List of Feelings Experienced

Adoration	Enraged	Jealous	Scared
Afraid	Enthusiastic	Joyful	Scattered
Anger	Envious	Lively	Secure
Annoyed	Excited	Lonely	Shy
Anxious	Exhausted	Loved	Smart
Ashamed	Furious	Loving	Sophisticated
Bliss	Flirtatious	Mad	Sorry
Boredom	Foolish	Mean	Strong
Bothered	Fragile	Minimized	Surprised
Broken	Frightened	Nervous	Suspicious
Cautious	Frustrated	Naughty	Terrified
Cheerful	Glad	Obsessed	Thrilled
Confident	Guilty	Obfuscated	Tired
Content	Greedy	Obliged	Unsure
Confused	Glutinous	Pleased	Upset
Curious	Happy	Pressured	Vivacious
Delighted	Hopeful	Proud	Vulnerable
Depressed	Hopeless	Perturbed	Victorious
Disappointed	Horrified	Regretful	Weak
Disgusted	Hurt	Relieved	Worried
Disturbed	Hysterical	Respected	Worthless
Embarrassed	Indifferent	Restless	Worthy
Empty	Infatuated	Risqué	
Energetic	Interested	Sad	
Enlightened	Irascible	Satiated	
Enlivened	Irritated	Satisfied	

Appendix C: Description of Healthy Sexual Feelings

exciting	determined	assertive
engaged	friendly	frisky
giving	forgiving	involved
agreeable	empathetic	pampered
loving	negotiable	passionate
mutual	pleasing	safe
reciprocal	responsive	trusting
sexy	voluntary	validating
indulged	cherished	seduced
stimulated	pleasurable	affectionate
tender	sensitive	considerate
captivating	aroused	concupiscent
boundaries	lustful	gratifying

Recommended Reading

"10 Ways Childhood Trauma Can Manifest in Adult Relationships," Psychology Today (Sussex Publishers, February 19, 2022), https://www.psychologytoday.com/us/blog/invisible-bruises/202202/10-ways-childhood-trauma-can-manifest-in-adult-relationships.

Tchiki Davis, MA, Ph.D. "List of Emotions: 271 Emotion Words" (+ PDF), Accessed March 10/2022, https://www.berkeleywellbeing.com/

Kendra Cherry, *The 6 types of Basic Human Emotions and Their Effect on Human Behavior*, April 5/2021, https://www.verywellmind.com.

Alan Cowen, *How Many Different Kinds of Emotion are There?* May 9/2018, https://www.frontiersin.org/

Nir Eyal, *20 Common Values and Why People Can't Agree on More*, www.nirandfar.com/common_values/

Mind Tools, "What are your Values? Deciding What's Most Important in Life. Decision Making," https://www.mindtools.com.

Brené Brown, *Atlas of the Heart -Mapping Meaningful Connection and the Language of Human Experience*, Random House Publishing Group, November 30, 2021.

Joseph Telushkin, *Words That Hurt Words That Heal*, William Morrow & Company, 1996.

Patricia Love, Ed.D. and Steven Stosny, Ph.D. *How to Improve Your Marriage without Talking about It*, Broadway Books, New York, 2007.

Gary Chapman, *The 5 Love Languages, the Secret to Love That Last*. Northfield Publishing 2015

Alex Comfort, MD, D.Sc. More Joy of Sex: A Lovemaking Companion to The Joy of Sex. Pocket Book 1994

Marcus and Ashley Kusi, Emotional and Sexual Intimacy In Marriage: How to Connect or Reconnect With Your Spouse, Grow Together and Strengthen Your Marriage. Our Peaceful Family, 2017

John Bradshaw, *Healing the Shame that Binds You*, Health Communications, Inc, 1988.

THANK YOU FOR READING
Head, Heart, Crotch Connections!

I hope you have found my book helpful for your HHC connection. If you have enjoyed the concepts I have introduced in my book, or they have helped you in some way, I'd love to hear about it! Head on over to Amazon to leave me an honest review. Your feedback will help make this book and my future books better.

Thank You!

Dr. René Gilberto Vázquez del Valle

Want to Connect?
You can reach me directly through the following sites:

Email: reneleo2@gmail.com

Website: renev.authorchannel.co

Facebook: René Vázquez del Valle, DSW

Instagram: @rene_vdelv

LinkedIn: René Vázquez del Valle, DSW, LCSW-R

I look forward to hearing from you!

Acknowledgments

First and foremost, above all else, I would like to thank God for the inspiration and courage he has afforded me throughout my life and in my professional career, as well as the resilience he granted me to write this book. It has been many years in the making, with a long hiatus in between writings, as I waited to learn more and more from the clients I have had the pleasure of treating psychotherapeutically. Without those years of practice and the multiple professional relationships I have experienced, I could never have finished this book.

I wish to acknowledge my loving, lifelong partner, P.B. Orenstein, who encouraged me to express my thoughts, believed in my work, and with whom my connections have flourished throughout the years.

I am lovingly grateful.

I wish to thank my many friends, colleagues and clients who have shared their wisdom with me about the nature of their relationship struggles.

I wish to thank Dr. Patricia Mackay, Ph.D., for having guided me in my clinical knowledge of treatment and how to work sensitively with trauma; Meryl Singer, LCSW, for guiding my understanding of both treatment and as a role model for leadership skills; Dr. Samuel Jones, DSW, for inspiring me to seek doctoral education; Wayne Santiago, M.A. for sharing his psychological insights and his expressive nature; and to all of them for the years of supervision they afforded me, influencing my thinking professionally, while working for 30 years at the Baltic Street Outpatient Clinic of South Beach Psychiatric Center. Thankful for all the individuals I got to work with at the New York State Office of Mental Health, SBPC, who in their own ways enriched my knowledge and inspired me professionally.

Additionally, I would like to thank Maria Schreiber, LCSW, Latino Support, P.C., LCSW, Dr. Joseph Faillace, Ph.D., Queens County Neuropsychiatric Institute, and Dr. George Dempsey, M.D., East Hampton Family Medicine, all for offering me insights and a place to practice my chosen profession. My gratitude to Pooneh M. who has been so supportive and helped me to overcome my wariness of social media.

I am grateful to have found Self Publishing School, without whose support this manuscript would perhaps have never been accomplished, and through the supportive impetus provided by my coach, Kerk Murray, who believed in the concept and provided me with ongoing inspiration.

A word of thanks to Jeannie Culbertson, The Noteworthy Mom, for her amazing editing skills, her sensitivity in considering the subject matter, and her guidance and support in developing this book.

About the Author

Dr. René G. Vázquez del Valle, DSW, LCSW received his master of science in social work at Columbia University and his doctorate in social welfare at the CUNY Graduate School and University Center. He worked for the NYS Office of Mental Health; was an adjunct associate professor at Long Island University; invited guest speaker at both the NYU School of Medicine, Dept. of Psychiatry, and CUNY Law School; and evaluated grant proposals for NYC HIV programs by the Ryan White Foundation.

Additionally, he served both as clinical director and team leader at the Baltic Street Clinic of South Beach Psychiatric Center, an outpatient ambulatory care clinic of the New York State Office of Mental Health. During his thirty-year tenure at SBPC, he engaged in clinical treatment, policy analysis, research, administration and developed a clinical treatment model for Spanish speaking patients.

He currently works as a clinical consultant and practitioner at the following clinics: Latino Support PC, Queens County Neuro-Psychiatric Institute, and the East Hampton Healthcare Foundation: Family Medicine clinic.

In his leisure time, he enjoys landscape design, swimming, film festivals, and international travel. He currently resides in Jackson Heights, Queens, NY, and East Hampton, NY, and works as a private practice therapist in several mental health clinics throughout the state.

Made in the USA
Monee, IL
18 February 2024